NO SALVATION

OUTSIDE

THE POOR

NO SALVATION
OUTSIDE
THE POOR

Prophetic-Utopian Essays

JON SOBRINO

ORBIS BOOKS

Maryknoll, New York 10545

Founded in 1970, Orbis Books endeavors to publish works that enlighten the mind, nourish the spirit, and challenge the conscience. The publishing arm of the Maryknoll Fathers and Brothers, Orbis seeks to explore the global dimensions of the Christian faith and mission, to invite dialogue with diverse cultures and religious traditions, and to serve the cause of reconciliation and peace. The books published reflect the views of their authors and do not represent the official position of the Maryknoll Society. To learn more about Maryknoll and Orbis Books, please visit our website at www.maryknoll.org.

Translation copyright © 2008 by Orbis Books.

Original publication: *Fuera de los pobres no hay salvación: Pequeños ensayos utópico-proféticos,* © 2007 by Editorial Trotta, Ferraz, 55. 28008 Madrid, Spain.

English translation published by Orbis Books, Maryknoll, NY 10545-0308.

Manufactured in the United States of America.

Library of Congress Cataloging-in-Publication Data

Sobrino, Jon.
  [Fuera de los pobres no hay salvación. English]
  No salvation outside the poor : prophetic-utopian essays / Jon Sobrino.
    p. cm.
   ISBN-13: 978-1-57075-752-5
   1. Liberation theology. 2. Salvation. 3. Catholic Church—Doctrines.
  4. Poverty—Religious aspects—Catholic Church. 5. Poverty I. Title.
  BT83.57.S69313 2007
  261.8'325—dc22
                          2007026901

To Pedro Casaldáliga
with gratitude and hope

Contents

Prologue   ix

1. **The Crucified People and the Civilization of Poverty**   1
   Ignacio Ellacuría's "Taking Hold of Reality"
       Taking Hold of Reality   2
       "The Crucified People"   3
       The Civilization of Poverty   9

2. **Depth and Urgency of the Option for the Poor**   19
       The Depth of the Option: Facing the Unfathomable
          Mystery of the Poor   20
       Saving the Poor   25

3. *Extra Pauperes Nulla Salus*   35
   A Short Utopian-Prophetic Essay
       The Need to Reverse the Course of History   35
       A World That Is Gravely Ill   37
       The Poor and Salvation   48
       Extra Pauperes Nulla Salus   69
       The Mystery of the Poor   72

4. **The Centrality of the Kingdom of God Announced by Jesus**   77
   Reflections before Aparecida
       The Centrality of the Kingdom of God   77
       Utopia   80
       The Centrality of the Poor in Christianity   88
       The Following of Jesus   90
       A Final Word   97

5. **The Resurrection of One Crucified**   99
   Hope and a Way of Living
       Death and Victims   99

A Drama in Two Acts   101
The Hope of the Victims   102
The Hope of Nonvictims   103
Living in Accordance with Jesus' Resurrection   105

6. **Helping Jesus' Legacy to Bear Fruit in the Churches**   109
   Ellacuría on Archbishop Romero
   The People   110
   God   116
   Following   121
   Grace   126

Notes   129

Index   143

Prologue

This book brings together articles written in the past several years. The underlying reflection is about our present world, a world of poverty and opulence, victims and victimizers; about the salvation and humanization that are so urgently needed; and about where that salvation and humanization might come from. They are all based on the words of Ignacio Ellacuría in his last speech, given in Barcelona on November 6, 1989, ten days before his assassination: "This civilization is gravely ill—sick unto death, as Jean Ziegler says; to avoid an ominous, fatal outcome, the civilization must be changed." With absolute and radical clarity Ellacuría added, "We have to turn history around, subvert it, and send it in a new direction."

Today's world, the official and politically correct world, refuses to listen, and in any case to take the radical action required by the utter gravity of the problem. An example from our own time: in Nairobi, where the World Social Forum has just ended, 2.6 million people—60 percent of the population—live in appalling shacks. In Kivera alone, eight hundred thousand people live with one sordid latrine for every two hundred people.

Some may say that in our official world we have already come out of the dogmatic sleep from which Kant sought to free us. But we have yet to awaken from the sleep of cruel inhumanity of which that sixteenth-century monk in La Española accused the landowners, perpetrators of cruelty and extermination, on the third Sunday of Advent, 1511: "Are these not human beings? Do they not have rational souls? Do you not see this? Do you not feel it? How can you stay in such lethargic sleep?"

Today as well there are a few prophetic voices, but not many; the rumor of misery and the cry of death filter through the drawn shades of indifference. Voices of hope can also be heard. Dom Pedro Casaldáliga, lashing out at this world of ours, also acknowledges that "humankind is moving, it is turning toward truth and justice; utopia and commitment are still very present on this disillusioned planet."

And the important thing is that we have this boundless hope, even if it remains hidden in and by our world: we can heal this, our civilization of capital and wealth. Ellacuría said that healing it will of course require all kinds of intellectual, social, and political effort. But we speak of boundlessness, because in opposition to the civilization of wealth he proposed the civilization of poverty—a surprising term that he often had to explain but never abandoned, in order to make clear that for the most part, the solution must be the opposite of the ones being offered now. In the same speech he simultaneously affirmed the hope and the scandal of the solution: "Only utopia and hope enable us to believe and encourage us to try, with all the world's poor and oppressed people, to turn history around."

These are the reflections we have brought together in the first three chapters of this book. In the following two chapters we analyze two fundamental realities from the biblical Christian tradition: the reign of God and the resurrection of the dead. They express the radical hope of our faith, the praxis that accompanies it, and the grace of the gift. They will serve well as theological background for the more historical reflections of these chapters, which seems important in our secularized societies—because globalization, democracy, and progress do not offer, even in a secular way, sufficiently radical symbols to guide human and social life in the direction of brotherhood.

In the last chapter we shall remember Archbishop Romero and Ignacio Ellacuría in an explicit and precise way: by remembering the most important words spoken by Ellacuría about Archbishop Romero. I think it also serves to illustrate the theme of the earlier chapters, although now the reflection becomes deeply personal. It is a small example, perhaps, of how to do the theology of witnesses, which cannot replace but enriches and deepens the theology of texts.

Readers will see that the book does not touch on present-day themes, such as interreligious dialogue, feminism, ecology, or bioethics, which is an obvious limitation. But it does not turn our reflections into relics of the past. Returning to Ignacio Ellacuría and Archbishop Romero, to Medellín and the Church of the poor, does not mean resorting to feel-good nostalgia or shamelessly chaining ourselves to a glorious past that is nevertheless past. I think it means returning to the deep well that still pours out living water, to a hidden root that still nourishes us, since there are as yet no other roots to replace it. I compare it to the Gospel of Mark, to which we must always return to refresh the exuberance of *euaggelion* and the reign of God, faith and following Jesus, and especially to discover the meaning of grace, costly grace, which we so often whittle down into cheap grace—not only in the religious context but in everyday life, trivializing it, reifying it, demystifying it.

In addition to all this, I have more specific reasons for remembering: in order to keep Archbishop Romero and Ignacio Ellacuría alive. It seems important to me to remember the real truth of Monseñor in order to keep him as he was and as he is remembered and loved by the poor and by honorable and generous men and women—not watering him down, as if that would lift him up onto the altars. Ellacuría still lives in many places: Ellacuría the philosopher—the sharp, critical, and independent thinker—and also the Ellacuría of praxis, able to enflesh the true reality of a suffering people in the university and place it at their service; Ellacuría the realistic negotiator, clinging to what is right and setting aside naïveté. But I think we must also remember what I have called the forgotten Ellacuría, man of the crucified people and the civilization of poverty, the follower of Jesus, who stood before the mystery of God, struggling with it as Jacob did. I consider it very important to remember the whole Romero and the whole Ellacuría, out of respect for them as persons, but also because I think such a historicized memory can bring only good to our present-day world. That is not taking refuge in the past, but bringing good seed to sow in the present.

The third chapter gives the book its title: *Extra pauperes nulla salus* (No Salvation outside the Poor). This is new, scandalous, and of course countercultural. The reader is left to judge whether it is rational or reasonable. For me, writing about it is always perplexing and discomforting. But I also hope that others will criticize, improve, and complete the task. Anyway I shall keep the title as a wake-up call, to take absolutely seriously the helplessness of our world and the seeds of salvation—often ignored, misunderstood, and unappreciated—that are to be found on the underside of history.

These reflections are based on theology, on data and analysis regarding the present world, and also on experience and faith. All together, especially where the *extra pauperes* is concerned, the reflection seems to me more mystagogical than autonomous and analytical. It is also negative theology, expressing what is happening to us. I think that in order to understand—or criticize—these writings, it will help to have the *esprit de finesse* that Pascal recommends.

I have tried to avoid repetition, but it has not always been possible. Perhaps the repetition will highlight the important parts, although even when repeated they should not be taken as common knowledge.

The reader will note that the book does not address specifically ecclesial themes. I can only say that the core of the presentation, the life and death of God's creation, with all its analytical limitations and needed corrections, can serve today as an *articulus stantis vel cadentis ecclesiai*.

As Archbishop Romero said, "*Gloria Dei vivens pauper*" (the glory of God is the poor person who lives). Today that is what is at stake. I am appalled to see that, apparently, no one is taking responsibility for the inhuman state of our world. No one is proposing the kind of conversion needed to change the world. One hopes the Church will set that example. One hopes it will happen in Aparecida [*the site, in Brazil, of the fifth meeting of the Latin American Bishops Conference in May 2007—eds.*]. The poor of this world will be grateful.

This book is dedicated to Bishop Pedro Casaldáliga. I met him in São Paulo, Brazil, in 1980, a month before the assassination of Archbishop Romero, about whom we talked at length. I dedicate it in gratitude for Don Pedro's word as a prophet, poet, and tireless bearer of *eu-aggelion*—gratitude, especially, for his life wholly given to all people, but always beginning with and through the weak and poor; and gratitude for his poem "San Romero de América," a work of universal inspiration and heartfelt love.

I dedicate it in the hope of being always in tune with the forever hopeful and hope-giving Don Pedro, with Jesus the Son and elder brother, and with the God who always embraces us and takes us by the hand. And finally, in the hope that humanity will be healed, that there will be salvation for the poor, that we too will miraculously let ourselves be saved by them, and become truly a human family.

January 2007
—*Translated by Margaret Wilde*

1

The Crucified People and the Civilization of Poverty

Ignacio Ellacuría's "Taking Hold of Reality"

I want to begin with some brief clarifications. I am not a Zubiri scholar. What I know of him I mainly learned through Ellacuría, not so much through his writings on Zubiri but from what we might call the Zubirian flavor that permeated his thinking. What I knew of Ellacuría's thinking was more the theological than the philosophical side. I saw in him the influence of Rahner, his theology professor at Innsbruck; a good measure of Marx; and a large measure—what is generally least noticed—of the biblical-Jesuanic tradition, the tradition of St. Ignatius of Loyola and Archbishop Romero. Finally, I believe the Salvadoran social reality, and sometimes the ecclesial reality, had a decisive impact and influence on his thinking.

In this essay I want to analyze two aspects of his vision of reality: "the crucified people" and "the civilization of poverty." Both themes are from his mature thinking, not passing youthful reflections, and Ellacuría considered them very important. Today, however, they are generally overlooked, except in some writings on his theology.[1] I don't know if this is true in the philosophical discussion, but it does happen when Ellacuría is spoken of in broader terms. This is the "forgotten Ellacuría," an understandable oversight, but an impoverishing and irresponsible one, because this countercultural Ellacuría can always be a Socratic gadfly: uncomfortable but positive, and necessary, in today's world.

It may be said that things have changed, and that Ellacuría himself

Presentation at the closing of the II Congreso Internacional de Filosofía Xavier Zubiri, held at the Central American University "José Simeón Cañas," June 21–24, 2005. Published in *Revista Latinoamericana de Teología* 66 (2005): 209–28.

would be on guard against the mimetic repetition of concepts; he would prompt us to historicize them. But I think we need to return to these themes, to unmask the reality that is still largely made up of crucified peoples, and to set our sights on a more human civilization which can still be described as a civilization of poverty.

Taking Hold of Reality

Ellacuría understood the formal structure of intelligence as "grasping and facing reality,"[2] which can be seen in three dimensions: "taking hold of reality" (the intellective dimension), originally from Zubiri, to which he added "bearing the burden of reality" (the ethical dimension) and "taking responsibility for reality" (the praxic dimension). To these I have added—more from experience and intuition than from theoretical reflection—"letting ourselves be carried by reality" (the dimension of grace), to which we shall return later on.

What first impacted me in Ellacuría's thought was his emphasis on taking responsibility for reality; it was early in the development of liberation theology, and the phrase came to define theology as the ideological moment in a praxis[3] aimed at "the greatest possible realization of the reign of God in history."[4] I tried to pick up that insight by defining theology as *intellectus amoris (iustitiae, misericordiae)*,[5] thus going beyond Augustine's *intellectus fidei*, and beyond *intellectus spei*, as Jürgen Moltmann reformulated it in 1978, in his *Theology of Hope*.

"Bearing the burden of reality" impacted me even more. Where I came from, it was totally new to hear—and perceive in the person of Ellacuría—that intelligence "has not been given to help people evade their real commitments, but to take on themselves the burden of things as they really are and with all that they really demand."[6] This means we cannot fully grasp reality without bearing it at its worst, which I think we still fail to understand. Ellacuría's death may well serve as a symbol of that burden-bearing. He thought about it and carried it to the very end. And it is not a coincidence that Salvadoran theology has led in the development of persecution and martyrdom as central themes, in theory as well as practice.

What was new to me was this understanding of the praxic and ethical dimensions of intelligence. But in the perichoresis of the diverse dimensions of intelligence, I also began to see the deepest implications of "taking hold of reality," which is not as simple as it seems. Ellacuría himself warned us of this. Taking hold of reality implies "being inside the reality of things—not only standing before the idea of things or their meaning—a 'real' being in that reality, actively, as opposed to a reified and inert way of being; it implies being among them through their active, material mediations."[7]

"The Crucified People"

When Ellacuría "took hold of the reality" of the Third World, he grasped it in an important way as a "crucified people." In 1977 he wrote a monograph that we came to know very well: "The Crucified People: An Essay in Historical Soteriology."[8] In 1981, on one of his exiles in Madrid, he re-emphasized that theme in a shorter article. Despite all the changes brought by subsequent years, those words are still lucid and even irreplaceable:

> Among the signs that are always appearing, some striking and others barely perceptible, there is an outstanding one in every age, in whose light all the others must be discerned and interpreted. That sign is always the historically crucified people, which remains constant although the historical forms of crucifixion are different. That people is the historical continuation of the servant of Yahweh, whose humanity is still being disfigured by the sin of the world, whom the powers of this world are still stripping of everything, taking away everything including his life, especially his life.[9]

From a theoretical theological perspective, the first text focuses more specifically on the relationship between crucified people and historical salvation, and the second on presenting it as reality, in which history is expressed with the greatest density, for which we must take responsibility and whose burden we must bear.

The Crucified People as Negativity: "Sign of the Times"

Ellacuría did not choose this language at random, or merely for its Christian resonance, because in his time it was not customary to apply to the "people" what we say of "Christ." He chose it intentionally to emphasize the negativity of reality; that was how he felt it and saw it, and that was central to all his thinking. In describing the role philosophy should play in de-ideologizing and unmasking the hidden reality, he challenged Heidegger: "Perhaps instead of asking why there is something rather than nothing, he should have asked why there is nothing—no being, no reality, no truth, etc.—where something should be."[10]

"The crucified people" does not express a random negativity, but a specific one. Economists and sociologists talked about a world of poverty and misery, of dependency, injustice, and oppression. But hardly anyone—except perhaps Archbishop Romero—described that reality as deeply as did the term "crucified people." Let us take a look.

Ellacuría used those words to give a name to great majorities. Thus the language of "people" and "peoples" is laced with death, not natural but historical death, which takes the form of crucifixion, assassination, the active historical deprivation of life, whether slowly or quickly. That death, caused by injustice, is accompanied by cruelty, contempt, and also concealment. I usually add that the crucified people are also denied a chance to speak and even to be called by name, which means they are denied their own existence. The crucified people "are not," and the affluent world prohibits or inhibits them from "becoming." The affluent world can thus ignore what happens to them, without any pangs of conscience.[11]

This crucified people, with all its negativity, is a "sign." Borrowing concepts from *Gaudium et Spes* 4 (1965), Ellacuría says that the crucified people are one of the main features of our time, not merely something factual that we may consider, but something central that must be considered, without which we do not have a full grasp on reality. But he went a step beyond the Council: he audaciously named the most important sign, around which the others revolve and make sense. This act of proclaiming the sign of the times had already begun, in a different way, at Medellín in 1968. There the bishops, foreshadowing Ellacuría's words quoted above, began with the following words:

> There are in existence many studies of the Latin American people. All of these studies describe the misery that marginalizes large masses of human beings in all of our countries. That misery, as a collective fact, is an injustice which cries to the heavens (*Justice* 1).[12]

The Crucified People as a Positive: "Bringers of Salvation"

Ellacuría knew well the biblical-Jesuanic tradition, in which negativity can reflect the positive. That is certainly true of the crucified Christ, acknowledged as Son of God and Savior, especially in and through the cross as we see in Mark 15 and 18. Closer to our theme, Isaiah presents in the songs of the servant of Yahweh (Isa. 52:13–53:12) a mysterious figure—real or imaginary, individual or collective—destroyed by the sins of the world and bringing salvation.

This servant is first of all a man of suffering, acquainted with infirmity, taken to his death—by the actions of others—without defense and without justice, despised and rejected by all. In the second place, he is not thought of as a possible savior but quite the contrary; he is seen as a leper, condemned, stricken by God and humiliated, and moreover as a sinner. They made his grave with the wicked and counted him among the transgressors.

Yet Isaiah audaciously attributes salvation to that figure of the servant, and Ellacuría also finds in it the basic elements for a historical soteriology in today's world: his innocent suffering and death bring salvation. It is said that the servant's state is not due to his sins, but he suffered without having sinned: he was crushed for our iniquities, wounded for the sins of the people. Thus, it is said, he shall make many righteous. In the language of our day, it is said that he will bring salvation to all, including his victimizers, because he has borne their iniquities. Says Ellacuría: "Only a hard-won act of faith could enable the singer of the servant to describe in this way what looks like just the opposite in the eyes of history!"[13]

With this servant in mind, and in terms of the hermeneutic circle, Ellacuría took hold of the reality of the Third World peoples, and also analyzed their salvific dimension. He saw the hope of liberation in the positive capacities of the people; thus, for example, with Archbishop Romero he defended and encouraged popular organization. But he also saw them in their negativity, as a suffering, "crucified" people, and that is what we focus on here. So that that word would not be in vain, he made an intellectual effort to historicize the content of the salvation brought by the crucified ones. Later we shall say more about the salvation that comes from below. For now let us remember two important, surprising, and overlooked elements of that salvation.

The crucified people offer light (Isa. 42:6 and 49:6 call the servant "light of the nations," although that song does not yet speak of the *suffering* servant). In our time, said Ellacuría, the Third World offers light to enable the First World to see itself as it truly is, which is an important element of salvation. He made the point with two graphic metaphors. He compared the crucified people to an inverted mirror in which a disfigured image shows the truth that the First World seeks to hide or dissemble. And in the metaphor of coproanalysis, an examination of feces, he showed that the existence of the crucified peoples reveals the true state of health of the First World.

A second element of salvation is hope. Ellacuría spoke of this twice in 1989. Out of its own suffering the Third World nourishes hope and offers it to a hopeless First World. Here is the full text of the first, transparently utopian comment:

All the martyrial blood spilled in El Salvador and throughout Latin America, far from leading to discouragement and hopelessness, infuses a new spirit of struggle and new hope in our people. In this sense although we are not a "new world" or a "new continent," we are clearly and verifiably—though not exactly by outsiders—a continent of hope, which is a very telling sign of the newness yet to come to other continents, which do not have hope but only fear.[14]

The second comment is from his last speech, on November 6, 1989:

There is a lot still to be done. Only utopianism and hope can enable us to believe and dare to try, with all the poor and oppressed people of the world, to turn back history, subvert it, and send it in a different direction.[15]

If we want to think about them, "truth" and "hope" are important salvific contributions of the crucified people. But they also contribute guiding energy to turn salvation in the right direction and work for it; they challenge our understanding of social, environmental, and religious salvation in a world that does not belong to poor people but creates them; and they help to unmask the dogma that a poor people can only receive but not give—which is vitally important to keep the affluent societies from falling into arrogance and dehumanization.

Ellacuría knows that the need to accept salvation—also—from below is not commonly recognized, not by philosophies, nor by ideologies, nor by theologies, although he mentions Marx's idea that there is a possibility of emancipation in the oppressed, "in the formation of a class of civil society that is not a class of civil society; of a class that dissolves all classes; of a sphere that possesses a universal character because of its universal sufferings and that demands no *special right* for itself, because it has not suffered any *special harm* but rather *harm, pure and simple.*"[16] This is an effort to think out the role of the weak (a social class, the proletariat, although the most disinherited are excluded) in historical salvation. The song of the servant is more radical, which is why Ellacuría uses it to formulate his understanding of reality.

The "Always" of the Crucified People

All this is astounding. But the "always" may be even more so: "that sign is always the historically crucified people, who not only remain but are *always* crucified in a different historical way." Is it responsible to say that? Today we can see a significant reduction of poverty and even dream of eliminating it, for example in China and India. But we must not forget the important, continuing setbacks in the struggle against poverty and the fact that relative poverty (the rich man and Lazarus), the terrible comparative harm between rich and poor, is not diminishing but increasing scandalously. In any case, Leonardo Boff is right: "When future generations judge our time they will call us barbarian, inhuman, and shameless, for our great insensitivity to the suffering of our own brothers and sisters."[17]

Personally I think that even from an analytical viewpoint, Ellacuría's "always" makes sense,[18] especially if the crucifixion of peoples is analyzed not only in terms of their unmet basic needs but also of the ignorance and indignity to which they are condemned, the depredation of their cultures, and the aberration of relative poverty in comparison with the affluent peoples. Things change, paradigms change. But we may wonder if there is not something trans-paradigmatic, if there are not principles of evil and sinfulness that run throughout history, with a dynamic of crucifixion that takes different forms but still produces death. That is what "always" means. And apparently it does exist.

Its Importance in the Present

People may say that, after all, "the crucified people" is only a way of speaking, but we must remember that we are engaged in a "language battle" in which enormous resources are invested. It is not the same to speak of "underdevelopment," let alone "developing countries," as to speak of "crucifixion." The first two are easily coopted. The third cannot be, so it is censored. Perhaps the language of "crucified peoples" will help to win the language battle, and thus the struggle for truth.

At a deeper level the affluent world, no matter how democratic, pluralistic, and global, needs to be shaken out of what Kant called "dogmatic sleep." The West is still largely sunk in "the sleep of cruel inhumanity," ignoring, suppressing, covering over terrible realities for which it is mainly responsible. The language of "crucified people" may help to shake it into wakefulness and action. That is what a Dominican friar, Antonio Montesinos, did in 1511 in La Española. On the third Sunday of Advent he confronted the landowners with the horrors they were committing and ended by asking them: "How can you stay in such lethargic sleep?"

This is also important from a theological viewpoint. The "signs" are mentioned again in *Gaudium et Spes* 11, this time not as characteristic of a time but as true "signs of God's presence or purpose"—signs in their historical-theologal meaning. For faith, the crucified people are in the place of God, in the same way that Paul and Mark, Bonhoeffer,

Moltmann, and others speak of a "crucified God." In any case, whether or not we accept this *theologoumenon*, reality is made present with radical ultimacy in the negativity of the crucified people, which at least protects the reality against trivialization.

Finally, "taking hold" of reality—specifically in its form as "crucified people"—points to the specific forms that should be used by the other dimensions of intelligence. Ellacuría thus intentionally formulated "taking responsibility for reality" as the praxis of "bringing the crucified people down from the cross." At the root of this idea is Ignatius Loyola's challenge to penitent sinners, to ask themselves in the presence of the crucified Christ: "what have I done, what am I doing, and what shall I do for Christ?" This means not only giving thanks for the forgiveness obtained, but doing, and then asking what to do. In the presence of the crucified people, Ellacuría historicized the answer to this question: "Bring them down from the cross."[19] He defined "bearing the burden of reality" as risk taking, persistence, and faithfulness to the end, and a willingness to die on the same cross with the crucified people.

"Letting ourselves be carried by reality," by the reality of the crucified people, points to a central paradox of Christian faith, although it may go beyond it. In theological language, it means that there is "grace" in the crucified people; that is, the crucified people bear us as their burden.[20] They do so in several ways: by giving us new eyes to see, new hands to work, broad backs to hold us up. And they give us hope. The only thing to say in support of this last point is that it happens. Obviously Archbishop Romero had to bear the burden of his people, but he also said that "with this people it's not hard to be a good shepherd [pastor]; they *move* one to service." Ellacuría rephrased Monseñor's words: "To complete what he said, we should add that 'with this pastor it is so easy to be the people of God.' "[21] The reality of the people bore up Monseñor, and the reality of Monseñor bore up the people.

To conclude this point, we can ask how Ellacuría came to this idea of "taking hold of reality," and to its formulation as "the crucified people." I don't have a self-evident answer, but I think it came from several sources. I believe Ellacuría allowed himself to be affected by the reality, out of his instinctive honesty toward reality, letting it be what it is—the secular Barthian version of the theologal "letting God be God"; and out of his real, not only conceptual, rootedness in a biblical-Jesuanic tradition that nourished him in the mystery of free will. This led to an uncommon "miracle." Clearly reality appeared to him as the crucified people. This is the *opthe* through which the appearances of the risen Lord are retold. There was gift and grace. Ellacuría responded and corresponded.

The Civilization of Poverty[22]

Unmasking the "Civilization of Wealth"

In his last years, Ellacuría was convinced of the need for "another" world—as we might say today—to keep us from falling into inhumanity, but not just any other world. We needed "to turn back history, subvert it, and send it in a different direction."[23] He called this the "civilization of poverty," and wrote about it three times,[24] to go beyond the prevailing civilization of wealth. He insisted on this to the end of his life; if the language is startling we might use the terms "solidary poverty" or "shared austerity," although Ellacuría preferred the word "poverty."

The civilization of wealth, says Ellacuría, offers development and happiness, and the means to attain them. The first of these "in the last analysis, proposes the private accumulation of the maximum possible capital by individuals, groups, multinational corporations, states, or groups of states as the fundamental basis of development."[25] The second proposes "the possessive accumulation, by individuals or families, of the maximum possible wealth as the fundamental basis of one's own security and the possibility of an ever-increasing consumerism as the basis of one's own happiness."[26] His judgment on that civilization is highly critical, but not simplistic:

> We do not deny that this kind of civilization, which prevails in both the East and the West and should be called a capitalist civilization—whether it is State or private capitalism—has brought some goods to humanity, or that these goods should be conserved and promoted (through scientific and technical methods, new forms of collective consciousness, etc.), but it has also brought greater evils and its processes of self-correction have not been enough to reverse its destructive course.[27]

The "greater evils" are that this civilization does not meet the basic needs of everyone, and as Ellacuría insisted with increasing force, that it does not build spirit or values that can humanize people and societies.

Regarding the life of the majorities, Ellacuría said there are not sufficient resources to extend to everyone the solution offered by the civilization of wealth—which in economic terms is called "the civilization of capital"—and that for this reason this civilization is also not ethical, in

Kantian terms. I do not know what Ellacuría would say today, in this time of economic globalization, when there are hints of a possibility of reducing poverty and making daily sustenance universal. But what is not becoming universal is the North American, European, or Japanese standard of living. They consume such a large part of the world's resources, raw materials, and energy that it will never be sufficient for the world population.[28]

Regarding spirit and values, this civilization is fundamentally oriented—and offers a spirit that clearly leads—to dehumanization. It is the civilization of the individual, of success, of the selfish good life. And the spirit is suffocated even more when the West that produced it understands itself not only as an achievement of talent and noble effort—which are very real in part, accompanied by a secular, gigantic historical depredation—but as the fruit of a kind of predestination similar to the age-old religious self-understanding of chosen peoples.

Let us focus on the United States, which behaves with all the naturalness and arrogance of those who follow a "manifest destiny." This nation is justified as an empire, considers itself sent into the world as missionaries of the wealth-god, and expects to be appreciated as a generous benefactor. People may say that there are also reactions against that self-understanding, but they are few and far between. And I do not know how willing such people are to give up the benefits of the civilization of wealth. This is true, in varying degrees, everywhere in the First World. This arrogant spirit is dehumanizing. By nature it tends to provoke contempt in some, and servility or irrational violence in others.

This conviction led Ellacuría to say that the United States "has a bad solution,"[29] which is worse than no solution, which is what the Third World has. In general, he said that the affluent countries "have no hope"—which the Third World does have—"but only fear."[30] Whatever improvements are made in reducing poverty, I personally do not see what meaning they can have in a world where equality and brotherhood are not among the guiding values of development. They can have no meaning if they constantly reenact the parable of the Rich Man and the Poor Lazarus—without narrowing, only widening, the separation between them, as the UN Development Program (UNDP) reports every year. Ellacuría's conclusion is clear: such a civilization is suffering a "humanistic and moral failure."[31]

Suspicions

Ellacuría not only unmasked the "great evils" of the civilization of wealth, against which it has not produced the necessary self-correcting mechanisms; he also unmasked what in the West is understood, in practice, without debate, as "goods." That led him to suspect that the West was ideologizing those goods in order to make them untouchable, beyond criticism. Two examples: his suspicion of democracy and even of human rights, which he wrote about in 1989.

For Ellacuría, democracy was obviously important, especially living under national security regimes. But in casual conversation he would say, for example, that "the United States values democracy and behaves democratically within its borders, but cares nothing about democracy outside those borders." This point is important, because the United States is not a *flatus vocis* but a very solid reality that has supposedly incarnated the very essence of democracy. Merely by sanctioning an absolutely antidemocratic inequality through its behavior, the inequality of "inside" and "outside," the United States engages not only in hypocrisy but in a conceptual contradiction. What El Salvador needed, Ellacuría said, was "not democracy [as offered in the propaganda], but human rights." In other words, the honest or hypocritical offer of democratic political superstructures did not guarantee the fundamental need: a just life.

But he also expressed this suspicion in theoretical terms: "The purpose of the ideologized manipulation of the democratic model is not the people's self-determined choice of a political and economic model, but to cover up the capitalist imposition."[32] Democracy has grave limitations: it expresses the political version of the civilization of wealth, and it can be manipulated, which is not surprising because it is created, as the theologians say. But if that manipulation is massive, if it leads to enormous cruelty, if it necessitates the institutional lie in the media and international forums, if it is practiced by the United States—the greatest and best expression of democracy—and above all if it keeps on happening, then the manipulation of democracy cannot be considered a mere accident; it seems to belong to the historical essence of democracy as it is practiced in the West, and more specifically, in relation to the poor majorities on the planet. We may well say that it also brought good things to the old colonies, or that it is the "lesser evil," but we should not ignore its great historical potential for dehumanization. Ellacuría's analysis was not based on the concept of democracy but on how it functions *in actu*, in and for the Third World, not in and for the limited area of the affluent countries. Therein lay Ellacuría's suspicions.

Let me mention one of Ellacuría's theological reflections in this context. When Vatican II spoke of the fundamental equality of all the members of the people of God, it was not only thinking of the early Church tradition; it was also inspired by central values of democracy and incorporating them into its doctrine. But Medellín went on to formulate a different theoretical concept of the Church: the Church of the poor. This went beyond the council's "democracy" and emphasized inequality within the Church, not in favor of the hierarchy but of the poor. Ellacuría deepened this new concept and affirmed that the poor belong at the center of the Church as a matter of structural, organizational, and missiological principle.[33] This approach did not go against the people of God, nor against the democracy it implies, but indirectly reveals a theoretical weakness with great practical consequences: in a world made up mainly of poor people, not even equality (if they had it!) would ensure that they would be taken seriously. They must be placed at the center in order not to be "expelled" from social and ecclesial citizenship. Ellacuría insisted on this for an evangelical reason: the poor can shape the church evangelically. From a social viewpoint, it follows that any society that claims to be truly "democratic" or egalitarian must be conceived and organized on the basis of the rights of the disadvantaged.

For Ellacuría, human rights are good; it was obviously necessary and urgent to put them in practice, and he worked toward that end. But in theorizing about human rights, he also expressed important suspicions: human rights are presented as essentially universal, but in fact they are not, not only because they are not yet real for everyone, but because in the real world, the fact that they are real for some people often means that they are denied and even violated by others:

> The problem of human rights is not only complex but ambiguous, because it not only brings together the universal dimension of humanity with the real situation in which people live their lives; it also allows those rights to be used ideologically, not only on behalf of human beings and their rights, but in the interests of one group or another.[34]

We cannot speak of the universal and nonideological validity of human rights without considering "whence" and "for whom" they are proclaimed:

> When a right is turned into a privilege, its universality is negated and it ceases to be a human right, becoming instead a class or group privilege.[35]

Two things are needed in order to de-ideologize human rights. One is dialectical historicization. Human beings are divided between those who enjoy rights and those who suffer them. "The dialectical reality between the strong and the weak, between the lord and the slave, between the oppressor and the oppressed, is more relevant to our problem."[36] The best way to identify an effective and dynamic right is thus "to powerfully deny that condition of weakness, slavery, and oppression."[37] And the dialectic must be upheld if the rights are to prevail. "The radical problem of human rights is the struggle of life against death, the search for what gives life in the face of what takes away life or produces death."[38]

The second thing needed is to historicize and prioritize the contents of those rights. Ellacuría insists on approaching them from the viewpoint of the fundamental meaning of life. The right to life above all, especially the life of the majorities and the peoples, must be seen historically in terms of the meaning of life.[39] Merely biological life "may be taken as self-evident in the wealthiest countries, where that right is guaranteed . . . but that is not true in most countries, either because of extreme poverty or because of repression and violence."[40] Thus, to proclaim the essential universality of human rights may be fallacious, irresponsible, and ideological, since "most of humanity . . . does not enjoy the real conditions for biological survival, because of hunger and unemployment."[41]

I would like to add, briefly, two other suspicions that, as I recall, Ellacuría expressed more implicitly. One is about freedom of expression, which is presented in essence as a right—a good thing, especially in our countries—but which does not always go together with the will to truth. Historically, it often doesn't. Indeed, freedom of expression may cover up the absence of a will to truth; thus, "the good" is placed historically at the service of "evil."

The other suspicion has to do with prosperity, which today means an eager, truly compulsive desire for a better life, for "unlimited" well-being, without considering that it may also be dehumanizing both for those who enjoy it and for those who pay the costs. This neurosis is also expressed in ostentation and Pharaonic behavior, in social and sometimes religious contexts: Singapore, world soccer championships, weddings, and so forth. This prosperity and ostentation are not motivated by a desire for humanization. They divert people's attention from the reality of the majorities who do not benefit directly from the deification of prosperity, toward the minorities who are presented as economic benefactors, the ones who make entertainment (that is, happiness) possible. In the face of the divinization of progress that they offer, it would be good to remember the reflections of Jürgen Moltmann on the future of the new millennium: "progress and precipice."[42]

Ellacuría was a prophet who denounced evils, but he was also suspicious and taught suspicion of that which may be good but is presented as indisputably good, since it can also be placed at the service of evil. He did so because he "took hold" not of just any reality, but also of the permanent reality of the crucified peoples—in spite of the progress and democracy around them, and in spite of the universal declaration that theoretically defends human rights.

Civilization of Poverty

The civilization of wealth does not "civilize." Ellacuría contrasted it with the civilization of poverty, to which he devoted a lot of theoretical analysis in his last years, even in the midst of all kinds of urgent needs. He considered this the way to historicize "the civilization of love" described by the popes. And he continued doing so right to the end, mostly alone, with one exception that I remember—Pedro Casaldáliga, who said: "To the 'civilization of love' we should add what the Jesuit, Spanish, Basque, Salvadoran theologian Ellacuría has felicitously described as 'the civilization of poverty.' "[43]

Let us begin with a clarification. Ellacuría obviously was not aiming for universal pauperization. He described the civilization of poverty in order to contrast it with the civilization of wealth. In a world sinfully shaped by the dynamic of capital and wealth, we need to develop an opposing dynamic that can salvifically overcome it. The thesis of a civilization of poverty thus "rejects the accumulation of capital as the engine of history, and the possession-enjoyment of wealth as the principle of humanization; rather it makes the universal satisfaction of basic needs the principle of development, and the growth of shared solidarity the basis of humanization."[44]

His positive programmatic affirmation, put simply, is this: the civilization of poverty is "a universal state of affairs which guarantees the satisfaction of basic needs, the freedom of personal choices, and an environment of personal and community creativity that permits the emergence of new forms of life and culture, new relationships with nature, with others, with oneself, and with God."[45]

Ellacuría said that this civilization of poverty is "based on a materialistic humanism, transformed by Christian light and inspiration,"[46] and I would like to add a word about that. The backdrop of the civilization of poverty and its humanizing potential is the biblical-Jesuanic tradition. We have already said that in Isaiah the crucified people can bring salvation, but more generally, all the Old and New Testament tradition focuses on the salvation that comes from the poor and the small: a childless old woman, the small people of Israel, a marginal Jew. . . . José

Comblin also sees a positive, joyful spirit in poverty that he contrasts with the spirit of wealth:

> In El Salvador I have seen shacks overlooking the ocean, where thousands of people live in precarious conditions—including the risk of falling into the water. But the people there live joyfully, with an awareness, openness, and patience that are the opposite of the world of the wealthy.[47]

We need to work to make that civilization of poverty a reality, or to make its elements a moving force toward a new reality. It is not enough to preach it as a prophecy against the civilization of wealth, or even merely to proclaim it as good news for the poor of this world. The solution "cannot be to withdraw from this world and confront it with a sign of prophetic protest, but to become engaged in it in order to renew and transform it into the utopia of the new earth."[48]

In this context, Ellacuría proposed two fundamental ways to undertake the transformation of the present civilization. The more understandable and acceptable of these, at least for some, is "to create economic, political and cultural models that can enable a civilization of labor to replace a civilization of capital."[49] The other is positively to strengthen "shared solidarity, a fundamental characteristic of the civilization of poverty, in contrast to the closed and competitive individualism of the civilization of wealth."[50] This solidarity is not only an important element for a priori thinking about the new civilization we seek, but a posteriori it brings in something fundamental from the Christian tradition and the best Latin American traditions, which can overcome tendencies of dissociative individualism.

To speak of solidarity takes us beyond instrumental effectiveness into a different plane of reality. It is to speak of "spirit," of spiritual effectiveness. This for me is the most striking part of Ellacuría's thinking about global social reality: his focus on the spirit that informs a new civilization, which can be generated by the poor above all:

> It is poverty that really leaves room for the spirit, which will no longer be stifled by the need to have more than the next person, by the greedy desire for superfluous things, when most of humanity lacks the basic necessities. Then the spirit can flourish, the enormous spiritual and human richness of the poor and the people of the Third World, which today is stifled by misery and by imposed cultural models that are more advanced in some aspects, but not more fully human.[51]

These are unforgettable words: "the enormous spiritual and human richness of the poor and the people of the Third World." He does not mean refusing to see the evils caused by poverty, a refusal uncharacteristic of Ellacuría. Describing in words what that spirit is is also hard; I am convinced that only those who have experienced it can talk, helplessly, about it. Put as simply as possible, many people find in the Third World "something" that they do not see in the world of wealth, and that "something" is of a higher quality.

Archbishop Romero attributed a special force to the people, to the popular majorities. "They *impel* one to serve them," he said in his Homily of November 18, 1979. Ellacuría was moved by Monseñor's vision of the people's "ability to find ways out of the gravest problems."[52] Having seen the Rwandan refugees from a distance, and many Salvadoran communities up close in times of war, earthquake, and everyday life, I have talked about their "primordial saintliness," their decisiveness in living and sharing life.[53] The term "quality of life" does not come from the world of the poor, because it presupposes life, which the poor cannot take for granted. But "life impulses" do come from that world, where life is not reified and contemplated within and for the sake of the consumerism of the civilization of wealth. From the poor come humanity, embrace, community, art, culture, theology.

Ellacuría was not simplistic or unjust. He knew and appreciated the advances of science and technology, which can be placed at the service of the human, and he also knew the cultural models and expressions of spirit in the West. Today we value tolerance and dialogue—although they too entail grave dangers when viewed unilaterally; there have also been advances in solidarity, although sometimes vaguely and even selfishly expressed, viewed unilaterally as aid to those who suffer rather than as a mutual giving and receiving from those who suffer.

But that is not enough. We need a new axis, around which the diverse elements that shape a society can revolve in human ways. The civilization of poverty, which comes fundamentally from the spirit of the poor—and the spirit of Jesus—generates values that, together with the most genuine civilizing traditions of the past and present, can create such a new axis. This would require us to reverse the dogma that the world only revolves around wealth.

It is hard to say what that axis, filled with a new spirit, might be, but perhaps the following may be elements of that spirit:

a. Being in reality, overcoming the docetism of living in unreality, in islands of affluence, alienated, detached from the poor and oppressed majorities.

b. Honesty toward reality, overcoming the lie and the cover-up with the will to truth, giving names to the millions of victims and martyrs, honoring their memory which nourishes us.

c. Compassion for the suffering of the great majorities, prophetically denouncing the injustice that produces it.

d. The demand for freedom by and for everyone, and understanding one's own freedom in a way that does not enslave, that does not prevent the doing of good.

e. Bearing the burden of history, every day until the end.

f. The joy of recognition that we are all brothers and sisters, which may lead to suffering but cannot be overwhelmed by sadness, and the celebration of that joy.

g. Caring for nature and all creation, within which we become a greater unity.

h. The utopian hope for a new heaven and a new earth.

i. Openness to an ultimate mystery in reality—and for some, coming out of ourselves, as in the prayer of Francis of Assisi, and giving a name (Father, Mother) to that mystery, without making God any less ineffable and mysterious.

At the end of the first section I described Ellacuría's words about the crucified people as astounding. The same, or more, is true of his words about the civilization of poverty. Let us end with some brief reflections, not to lessen the impact but perhaps to understand it.

In the first place, Ellacuría knew the great evils that occur in the world of poverty—the evils committed by the poor, their human condition, the evil inclinations caused by unmet needs, the dehumanization that comes from the civilization of wealth—lead them in large part by force or deception to commit evil. He was not naïve. But he saw no other way, besides the spirit that rises out of the civilization of the poor, to overcome the greater dehumanization of the civilization of wealth. And he was positively captivated by their creativity, their generosity, their persistence, their solidarity, their austerity, their hope, their openness to transcendence.

Second, Ellacuría knew that history does not move without power. In his time, in the midst of the people's struggle to build a new society, he recognized the need for and the legitimacy of the political front that sought power, but he gave priority to the organization of the base (grass roots), which did not seek to come to power. "The social is more basic than the political," he said.[54] I think he would emphasize this in building the civilization of poverty. In this sense, Ellacuría did not slip into "messianism," as is sometimes alleged of the liberation theologians, although he valued the messianic aspect of the biblical-Jesuanic faith: that is, upholding the hope of the poor, but through patient work. Perhaps he was influenced by the fact that in El Salvador the revolution had not triumphed as in Nicaragua; rather, the building of a new society always went against the established powers. The theologians, priests, and pastoral agents of a new society never held power, nor were they favored by those in power, as was the case, more or less, in Brazil and Nicaragua.

Finally, let us ask where he came upon the idea of upholding utopia and expressing it as "the civilization of poverty." Ellacuría was always obsessed by *justeza*, that is, adjusting to reality and its real possibilities. He was also realistic in doing everything possible so that reality would give more of itself. That did not make him an opportunist, or even a mere "possible-ist." He also believed in the need for prophecy and utopia in order to move history forward. So where did this utopia come from? It undoubtedly had personal roots, but we must emphasize an objective and historical element that he himself identified: "Some places are more propitious than others for the emergence of prophetic utopians and utopian prophets."[55] Specifically, the place where it is possible to think of the "civilization of poverty" is not the world of affluence, where the individual, success, and the good life are exalted. Even less is it the world of arrogant power: "We are the reality." It is in the Third World, where prophecy and utopia seem necessarily to come together, where injustice and death reach intolerable levels, and where hope seems to be the quintessence of life. This is the world in which Ellacuría was consciously engaged.

I don't know what Ellacuría would say today, in times of globalization and postmodernity. For myself, I would like to close by expressing a conviction and a desire. The conviction is that "they killed Ellacuría for confronting the civilization of wealth," and the desire is that "we not let him die for defending the civilization of poverty."

—Translated by Margaret Wilde

2

Depth and Urgency of the Option for the Poor

I have been asked for some reflections on the option for the poor, its complexity, and its meaning for the mission of the Church. Based on my experience in El Salvador in the past thirty years, I think it is important to emphasize two points. The first is the depth and urgency of what the Church must do for the poor, which is the most common approach and the one we focus on in this essay. The second is what the poor can do for the Church—and more radically, for the society; this approach is less common and is discussed in the next essay.

Understood in both directions, the option becomes a way to move toward a truly human and inclusive globalization that does not paradoxically become antihuman and exclusive. This may be an important step toward building the human utopia: "that the world may become a home for humanity" (Ernst Bloch). To put it in dynamic terms, this option would mean "turning back history, subverting it and sending it in a different direction" (Ignacio Ellacuría), or "humanizing humanity" (Pedro Casaldáliga).

But first I want to reflect on the depth that "the option for the poor" had at the beginning, which has diminished since then. In the form of a thesis, this depth clearly comes from the fact that it is an option for the poor. In them the mystery of reality breaks through [irrupts], and as the liberation theologians have repeatedly said, in them the very reality of God breaks through. Furthermore, since God desires their salvation and liberation and makes an option for them, our option for their salvation and liberation is an expression of our deification. When God opts to allow us to give salvation and liberation to the poor, it shows that we are graced by a God who is scandalously present in them. I also want to emphasize that "the option for the poor," although costly, should not

---

Published in *Revista Latinoamericana de Teología* 60 (2003): 283–307.

only be seen as implying suffering and risks, including martyrdom; it also gives meaning and joy to our existence. In recent decades I have personally been able to live in a Church that made a very profound option for the poor, and I have never seen so much joy in a Church.

The Depth of the Option:
Facing the Unfathomable Mystery of the Poor

In theologal terms, the poor give historical ultimacy to the mystery.

We cannot by any means take for granted that "the option for the poor" is *in possesione*, in Churches and theologies, needing only to be updated from time to time. In my opinion that is not the case; there has been progress in understanding the option, but little evidence of its being taken seriously. Clearly this option is part of the earliest Christian mystery, and is always in danger of being watered down and manipulated. Let us look at it more closely in the Gospel of Mark.

How to live Christianity was not at all obvious to Mark, even after several decades of Christian life in the communities. It was not obvious to the religious men of his time, or to Jesus' family members, or to his disciples. The women understood it better, although at the end, beside the tomb, even they were at a loss for words and had to fall silent.[1] The question "What does it mean to be Christian?" turned out to be not only costly but scandalous and countercultural; as we know, a less scandalous ending (Mark 16:9–20), easier to interpret in the communities, was added years after the Gospel was written. We can see that being Christian was not *in possesione* from the beginning.[2]

Something like this is true of the option for the poor. It has not been easy to live it over time and consistently, and it cannot be taken for granted as something obvious. The need to add the words "preferential," not "exclusive" or "excluding"—as reasonable as they are—is analogous to the reason for the new ending in Mark: to reduce the sharpness of the original ending.

The difficulty of maintaining the option is obviously its costliness, but the problem also comes—at the metaphysical level, we might say—from accepting and maintaining the understanding that a mystery is made present in the poor; some might say, *the* mystery. Historically, "reality has broken through" in them. Theologally, "God has broken through" in them. So, the mystery has broken through. We know it is not easy to accept any mystery, because if we take it seriously and not simply as an enigma, a mystery is unmanageable, especially when it is made present in the poor. Then it is not only unmanageable, but counter-cultural.

We begin with this reflection in order to place and hold the poor in the context of the mystery of God—and God in the context of the poor—at least when we look at the poor from the viewpoint of faith and theology.[3] This consideration is especially important from a pastoral viewpoint, because Churches tend to trivialize the poor and the mystery, or domesticate them, by means of innumerable doctrinal formulations. When the option for the poor is upheld at all, it is transplanted to the pastoral sphere; its deep roots in the faith are seldom maintained.

Praxis: The Poor Give Ultimacy to the Mission of the Church

The mystery of the poor is prior to the ecclesial mission, and that mission is logically prior to an established Church. What Jürgen Moltmann wrote many years ago is still true: "It is not the Church that 'has' a mission, but the reverse; Christ's mission creates itself a Church. The mission should not be understood from the perspective of the Church, but the other way round."[4] It is not that the Church already existed, and later asked what to do for and with the poor, as if the Church were formally established prior to its relationship with them, or as if its way of carrying out that option were unrelated to the essence of the Church, which remains unchangeable throughout history.

There are realities in the Church that precede its option for the poor—God, Christ, and the word, certainly—and we must hold central the truth that the initiative comes from above, from the God who "first" loved us. But the mystery of God and Christ is being revealed in relationship with the poor of this world, so that by deepening our understanding of the historical figure of the mystery of the poor, we are deepening our understanding of the mystery of God,[5] and vice versa. The option for the poor is thus decisive for the historical essence of the Church of Jesus. It follows that "facing" the poor does not express the categorical *ubi* of a substance called the Church, which was already in existence. Here, I believe, lies the radical and complex character of the option for the poor from the Church's viewpoint: the option fundamentally shapes its mission, and therefore its historical identity.[6]

We emphasize this because these days there are many doctrinal texts on the Church, but no forceful attention to the mission that must constantly re-create the Church. The option for the poor, as a reality, has done that in the past; in the present it has been diluted as a "fundamental" option, and the undeniably legitimate debate over whether it is a "preferential" but "not exclusive" option has not helped to restore its previously fundamental character. Many other things are offered to the Church these days, as if they were adequate guiding principles. These include, at the pastoral level, achieving critical mass (membership, documents, congresses, celebrations, canonizations, radio and TV media)— in other words, a successful pastoral ministry. The doctrinal level presents an all-embracing, rigid, clear, and distinct doctrine, which the institution believes will best express faithfulness to God and Christ. Some of this may be important, but I believe the fundamental direction of the mission has been lost, because the centrality of the poor in that mission has been diluted. That was not always the case, as we may recall even from before the historic 1968 meeting of Latin American bishops at Medellín. At the end of the first session of Vatican II, Cardinal Lercaro lamented that "something has been missing so far in the council," and he asked, "Where shall we find that vital impulse, that soul, let us say that fullness of the Spirit?" He replied, "This is the hour of the poor, of the millions of poor who are everywhere on the earth."[7]

Diversity and Depth of the Poor

We conclude this section with a matter that has been debated in recent years: there are different types of poor people, and we must consider the ways they have been discussed in theology, including the theology of liberation.

Above all we must distinguish between the diversity of the types of poverty, as they have appeared or are perceived, and the human, anthropological, and social depth of each poor person and of poor people as a whole. All this makes up the "world of poverty," and we can understand it more deeply by seeing it separately and in contrast with the "world of affluence."

Obviously there are different forms of poverty. In the Palestine of Jesus' time, for example, the poor could be described as follows: the socially excluded (lepers and mentally handicapped), the religiously marginalized (prostitutes and tax collectors), the culturally oppressed (women and children), the socially dependent (widows and orphans), the physically handicapped (deaf and mute, crippled and blind), the psychologically tormented (spirit-possessed and epileptic), and the spiritually humble (simple, God-fearing people, repentant sinners).[8]

Today this needs to be reformulated in part, but some things remain constant: there are majorities of human beings for whom life itself is a heavy burden, not only because of their natural limitations, but also for historical reasons. The depth of poverty is expressed in this burden. It affects the poor themselves in the first place, but it also affects those who generate the poor and act as spectators. In the biblical and Jesuanic tradition—as distinct from the Greek, Roman, democratic, and Western tradition—this depth leads to another depth: the depth of the mystery of God (and idols), of grace (and sin), of salvation (and condemnation).

In my view, this depth was the most important discovery of Medellín and the theology of liberation (which are used here as symbols to mark the place where history spoke up after centuries of silence). That is where a qualitative jump occurred ("God is the God of the poor"), as well as an epistemological break ("God is known through the poor"). In biblical language, there was a *kairos*. I am surprised how quickly people have come to say that we have gone beyond Medellín,[9] when obviously common sense and the Gospel of John should tell us that "the Spirit will guide you into all the truth" (John 16:13). Even more surprising is the almost absolute silence on Medellín by progressive theologians in the affluent countries, who still rightly invoke Vatican II, but often in a reductionist way, invoking it alone; and in a bourgeois way, rightly invoking it to demand their own rights within the Church, but without giving appropriate consideration to Third World poverty.

The first thing Medellín rediscovered was the depth of the poor, but let us now look at their diversity. I view it as a great achievement, especially in the Third World, to have understood the diversity of poverty and the specific depth of each of its expressions: Indians and Afro-Americans, gender, woman and Mother Earth, religions, and so on. Each of these has spoken up, and that is an important event. The hierarchy has also gradually incorporated it in Puebla and Santo Domingo [meetings of the Latin American bishops in 1979 and 1992], albeit more at the level of orthodoxy than of orthopraxis.

There is debate over the way in which liberation theology has addressed the diversity of poverty, and I would like to comment on it personally along the lines of Gustavo Gutiérrez. He obviously accepts advances in the understanding of the diversity of the poor, and recognizes that "valuable contributions have enabled us in a particularly fruitful way to go into some key aspects of that complexity."[10] But he still insists on the insight of Medellín, I think on principle and not in order to defend the origins of the theology of liberation. It was there that the reality of poverty spoke up and showed its depth, and we must uphold this, because today as in the past, "Poverty . . . issues a radical and all-encompassing challenge to human conscience, and to our understanding of Christian faith."[11]

This has never meant that we should develop a chemically pure concept of poverty as a genus to be divided, according to the old logic, into distinct species. But we do believe that the generic term "poverty," with all its historical fluidity, is irreplaceable as an expression of the denial and oppression of humanness, an expression of the need, the contempt, the voicelessness, and anonymity that millions of human beings have suffered. In one way or another it includes all the categories of poverty. Each one adds a unique dimension, a nuance of depth, that gives new meaning to the term "world of poverty," especially in its dialectical relationship with the "world of wealth."

Thus we must keep in mind all the expressions of poverty, and Gustavo Gutiérrez reminds us that this was always true. "From the beginning, the theology of liberation has been aware of the different dimensions of poverty. To say it in other words—as the Bible does—liberation theology has always been careful not to reduce poverty to its economic aspect, although it is a key aspect."[12]

Today we must explicitly name the diverse expressions of poverty as they become visible, each according to its own dynamic. But with respect to the charge that liberation theology was focused only on the economically poor, it seems important to me to remember two things. One is the past and present horror of cruel poverty, in the form of hunger and hunger-related illnesses, which kill 50 million persons every year. The other is that, etymologically, "economics" refers to the *oikos* of human life: not only living in an *oikos* as a physical place, but living it as an *oikos*, as a nucleus of humanity. In this sense, economic poverty expresses a deep human, anthropological, and social need: the difficulty of forming a home, human life, an *oikos*.

Coming back to the diversity of poverty, I remember the impact I felt twenty years ago from what the African theologians were saying: "We are suffering anthropological poverty; they have deprived us of our being." This statement has given rise to a Christian outcry unlike that heard in other places. The following passage from Engelbert Mveng seems to me more important than thousands of essays on the diverse forms of poverty:

What is the Good News of Jesus Christ for the victims of anthropological annihilation and impoverishment? . . . Amid the dismay of a world dominated by the noisy confrontation of hegemonic blocs, in the heart of a Church bewildered by the hubbub of the western communications media and the tumult provoked by apocalyptic prophecies at the end of the twentieth century . . . it is hard for humble African Christians to concentrate on the issues that matter most to them. The hour of face-to-face encounter with Jesus Christ is at hand. . . . When the day of truth comes, all those noises fade and we are left alone, crucified with Jesus Christ. Then a single cry goes up from our crosses to his cross. . . . My God, my God, why have you forsaken me? "God speaks; we must answer," and Africa is questioning God; God must answer. The real dialogue has begun.[13]

I confess that even after having shared the Latin American experience, I have only gradually begun to hear and understand the cries of women, indigenous people, and Afro-Americans. And I believe those cries have not only added—horizontally, we might say—new varieties or species of poverty; they have also enriched its depth: they have broadened and deepened the mystery of the poor.

My point is simple but important. We need to hold the diversity and the depth of poverty in a mutual relationship, and do theology in this way. We must also avoid letting diversity lead to factionalism.[14]

Theologally the tension between depth and diversity, albeit *sub specie contrarii*, leads us into the unfathomable mystery of God (depth) and prevents us from building a monolithic image of God (diversity).

Saving the Poor

There is no need for an extensive description of poverty in Latin America and the world. It is a world of "Lazaruses." This statement is true in the absolute meaning of poverty: 1.3 billion human beings must live on less than a dollar a day, which is a grave evil for the human species. In theological language this is the "macroblasphemy" of our time, as Casaldáliga put it, and for believers it is a low point as deep as the cross: "My God, my God, why have you forsaken me?"

Those "Lazaruses" coexist with "rich men." The reports of the UN Development Program have lost their impact, because they are now routine: in 1960 there was one rich person for every thirty poor people; in 1990, one for every sixty; in 1997, one for every seventy-four. This is the relational meaning of poverty.

Perhaps one example from the soccer industry will shake the conscience awake; this doesn't happen often because that industry, and more generally the sports and entertainment industries, are relatively immune to any critique of the capitalism that infects them. But the three best-paid soccer players in the world—an Englishman, a Frenchman, and a Brazilian, who all play on the same Spanish team—earn US $42 million a year; by comparison the San Salvador metropolitan area, with 1,821,532 inhabitants, has an annual budget of $45.6 million. This is comparative harm, a shameless insult to the poor, a failure of the human family. In theological language it is the failure of God in creation.

So we have poverty in both the absolute and the relative sense, expressed in different ways and different degrees, depending on whether the poor are peasants, women, indigenous, and so on. In an effort to synthesize, perhaps we can say that the poor are *the deprived and oppressed, with respect to the material basics of human life*; they are *those who have no voice, no freedom, no dignity*; they are *those who have no name, no existence.*

We often say this last, but it is worth repeating: *the poor don't exist.* What in the present world is *in possesione* is their nonexistence; above all, Africa does not exist. It is "the invisible continent," where "the war is not televised." The tragedies of Nicaragua and Haiti do not exist, the street children. . . . We have come a long way from Heidegger's admiring question: "why is there being instead of nothingness?" Now it seems there is "nothing," and that provokes nothing, no indignation, no protest. If that is so, we can express the essential forms and meaning of the option for the poor, positively and dialectically, in the following way.[15]

Mercy-Justice: Saving from Death

Saving from death is the central demand for all human beings. In Christian terms it is the fundamental way to be in tune with the God of life; Archbishop Romero said insightfully, "The glory of God is that the poor live," and these words can be taken as a "summary" of Christianity. They express the essence of what is at stake in the option for the poor.

But it is not easy to uphold the centrality of the poor, their suffering and their closeness to death. We need to reflect on this in thinking about the option for the poor. The Churches have always had some interest in the poor, but these days they do not make it a central and decisive reality, nor do they risk much for its sake. In addition to costliness and risk there is a serious theoretical problem, as Metz has stressed. His thesis is that "Jesus did not look first at the sin of others, but at their suffering."[16] But "Christianity very soon had serious problems with that fundamental sensitivity to the suffering of the other, which is inherent in his message. The disturbing concern for justice for the innocent person who suffers, which is at the heart of the biblical traditions, was too quickly transformed into concern for the salvation of sinners."[17]

This means making mercy the principal motive and guide in the mission of the Church; saving the poor from the slow death of poverty, or from the quick death of violence, repression, or war as the case may be, becomes the force that moves the Church to praxis and the guide that orients that praxis. And since poverty and suffering are massive and have historic causes, mercy must be historicized as a struggle against injustice, in favor of justice.

This is fundamental in the option for the poor as a praxis, and the theology that informs it must be understood as *intellectus misericordiae, iustitiae, amoris,* as the intellectual response to *misericordia, iustitia, amor quaerens intellectum.*

Prophecy and Word: Saving from Indignity

It is scandalous—and an expression of a great sin of concealment— that "the most real reality" in our world, what most touches God's heart, is the least-known reality, and thus the one that exists the least. Our awareness of that reality bears absolutely no relation to its massiveness, its "cruelty," nor as we shall see, its "saintliness." There is freedom of expression, we say, but there is not a will to truth; there are a thousand ways to keep poverty from saying its word, a thousand ways to render the poor voiceless. Some of these ways are shocking (killing the prophet); some are ordinary (denying the poor access to the communications media because they have no money); some are fallacious ("in the coming world of globalization, everyone will be able to speak").

This scandal of rendering reality voiceless reminds me of Rahner's words: "Reality wants to have a word (a turn to speak)." Reality is struggling, we might say, to let the voiceless say a word. This describes, albeit abstractly, something central to the mission of the Church: giving word to reality. Archbishop Romero, guardian of reality, also wanted to be a guardian of the word, so he said: "These homilies attempt to be the voice of this people. They want to be the voice of the voiceless. So they are doubtless bothersome to those who have too much voice."[18] Giving word thus means struggling against the concealment of reality, which is another way of describing "prophetic denunciation."

Prophetic denunciation is mostly unknown in today's Church, having been replaced in the best of cases by ethical judgments on neoliberalism, the war, and so forth. Ethical judgment is good, but ethics is not the same as prophecy, social doctrine is not the same as prophetic denunciation, and it is not sufficient in any case, because the word that only expresses principles is easily coopted.

Nor is denunciation the same as "protest." There is nothing wrong with protest (although there is some truth to the modern saying, "There is a proposal behind every protest"),[19] just as there is nothing wrong and much that is understandable about "venting," as everyone knows who has experienced lasting and helpless suffering. Denunciation means bringing to light the evils of reality, its victims and its perpetrators. Prophetic denunciation has ultimacy, because it is done "in God's name"; and as denunciation it is compassionate, because it is done against the perpetrators, but in defense of the poor. That is why Archbishop Romero gave voice to the poor. And because his word was true, he used it to defend the poor, since—as history has clearly shown—the truth is "in favor of the poor"; indeed amid so much impunity, corruption, and falsehood, it is often the only thing the poor have in their favor. Finally, denunciation is full of risks because it is annoying; that is why it is seldom maintained for long but falls into disuse.

I would like to add something else that matters to the poor when they are victims of violent death or disappearance. The truth restores dignity to the victims in the midst of diabolical distortion. Often they are not merely ignored, but accused of being victimizers. Archbishop Romero was accused of subversive agitation, and some said he "got what he deserved." The victimizers are even seen as victims: the soldiers and officers of criminal armies are said to be innocent victims, assassinated by terrorists or communists—sometimes under the orders of Medellinist priests. Overcoming this degradation of the truth means taking a step toward humanization. The truth becomes a reparation to the dignity of the victims. It recognizes their rootedness in a tradition of good and noble people, with high ideals, even with the generosity of having given their life for others.

Prophecy—giving a word, speaking the truth—is an essential part of the option for the poor. This transforms theology into *intellectus veritatis*.

Giving a Name: Saving from Nonexistence

It is said that in feudal times there were serfs, and in the Industrial Revolution there was a proletariat; we recall that their lives were cruel, but visible. Today the poor are invisible. We talk without even blinking about the excluded ones, for whom there is no room: the highest irony and hypocrisy of globalization, in which by definition there should at least be room for everyone. The logical result of invisibility is insensitivity, which relegates the poor to their natural place, as Aristotle would describe it: a distant, vague horizon, without a face, something between unreal and ghoulishly exotic—a kind of modern *sheol*. This is nonexistence.

For example, the poor don't even have a name. This is true in life, and has been well analyzed. But also in death, even when death is massive, unjust, and arrogant; in wars, genocide, and terrorism; by foot soldiers and especially, we must insist, by the state. Most of the North American victims in Vietnam have names carved on monuments; that may also happen with the victims of September 11, 2001, in New York, Washington, and Pennsylvania. But the street children, and many of the victims and the disappeared in Latin America, do not have names.[20] They also do not have a calendar. September 11 exists by its own, unarguable right; we need say no more. But October 7, 2001, the day the bombing of Afghanistan began, does not exist; nor does March 19, 2003, the day the war on Iraq began. And don't even mention December 11, 1981, the day the U.S.-trained Atlacatl battalion murdered about 1,000 people in El Mozote, El Salvador, including 160 children with an average age of six. In this context, giving a name means making things real, calling them into existence, as we know from Genesis.

The Churches may be doing something similar to those killed in massacres, the poor and defenseless majorities, many of them Christians, sometimes highly committed Christians. There have been noteworthy martyrs in Latin America, but mostly there have been thousands of men and women, children and old people, innocent, defenseless victims of persecution and repression, massively and cruelly massacred. In several places there has been a powerful effort to keep and honor their names; the popular communities and some Churches should take pride in that effort. But as a whole and officially, the institutional Church does not know what to do with them. It does not even have a name for those Christians (and non-Christians) who have died a historically cruel death, very close in Christian terms to that of the servant of Yahweh.

They are not usually called martyrs, although as we shall see there have been some exceptions. Certainly theology has moved forward significantly in its understanding of martyrdom, so that apart from the canonical definition, we now say that martyrs are not only those who die "for their faith," but also "for justice." The greatest change in the concept of martyrdom has been thinking of it as living like Jesus, furthering the cause of Jesus, the reign of God, engaging in conflict and struggle against the anti-kingdom, and for that reason being killed as Jesus was. These are the people we call Jesuanic martyrs.

But since these important advances are theoretical, the most painful aspect of the reality is still overlooked in all its enormity and cruelty: those massive deaths. The Church has even considered treating the death of soldiers and combatants as martyrdom—the reflection of St. Thomas,[21] now considered a *quaestio disputata*, is relevant here—but it does not know what to do with the innocent victims of massacres except by remembering the "holy innocents," a *theologoumenon* that has remained as a tragic ornamental-theological element of the stories of Jesus' childhood, which is to say that the matter is not taken seriously. In this context it seems very important to me that the millions of impoverished and massacred people be given names. The most important thing that Archbishop Romero did to conceptualize this fact from a pastoral perspective, and Ellacuría from a theological perspective, was to call attention to this anomalous and scandalous situation, and make reparation for the sin of dishonesty and ingratitude. And they gave names, "titles of dignity" as in Christology, to those massacred majorities: the "suffering servant" (Isa. 52:13–53:12), "Christ crucified in history," "the crucified people." Beyond the problems of language, beyond the possibility of making intelligent use of analogy, in order to understand those majorities "canonically" or at least "theologally" as martyrs, we must stress the decisive point: their likeness to Christ. Those majorities unjustly bear the burden of a sin that has been gradually destroying them in life, and has permanently annihilated them in death.[22]

God looks on them with infinite tenderness, but a most un-Christian silence has fallen upon them, a silence that is also felt when the great saints are proclaimed—"elitistically," if that word will not be misunderstood, which a Francis of Assisi or an Archbishop Romero would quickly and energetically protest. A new record of beatifications and canonizations was set in the pontificate of Pope John Paul II, but not one of the men and women who were murdered in the Third World for practicing justice, defending the poor, or being faithful to Jesus has been recognized by the Vatican. It goes without saying that the crucified peoples in Africa, Asia, and Latin America have gone unrecognized. At the solemn ecclesiastical level too, they remain nameless.

Now thanks to Archbishop Romero, Bishop Juan Gerardi,* and Don Pedro Casaldáliga the victims have a name, and that is a fundamental expression of the option for the poor. Just by mentioning the names of the tortured, dead, and disappeared, we recognize their fundamental dignity as human beings who deserve to be remembered as such. It may seem like a small concession, but it is the most important: to give existence to the victims is to give them the fundamental human right, in life or posthumously.

---

*Bishop Gerardi of Guatemala oversaw the Recovery of Historical Memory Project, which documented the history of human abuses in his country. He was assassinated in 1998 immediately after the release of the four-volume study.—*Eds.*

Framing the Option: Dialectic, Partiality, Engagement, Humility

The option for the poor must be carried out within a specific framework. In today's world, I would like to insist on four elements.

The first is the *dialectic* element. So much is said these days about dialogue, negotiation, and tolerance, and confrontation is so carefully avoided, that it's as if the poor had fallen from the heavens (or given the horrors of this world, perhaps we should say come up out of hell)—as if the problems could be resolved by some invisible hand reaching out to break down the egoism of the powerful and soften the edges of structural injustice, lies, and violence. Seen this way the option for the poor would not require a dialectic, a confrontation with the oppressor, least of all with the structural forms of oppression. Instead we try to avoid it.

In this situation we must remember the fundamental biblical and historical truth that was so often proclaimed at the time of Medellín and Puebla: "There are rich people because there are poor people, and there are poor people because there are rich people." I was happy to read these words of José Comblin recently: "In reality, humanity is divided between the oppressors and the oppressed."[23] Of course, we must avoid and control violence as much as possible, but an option for the poor that fails to be dialectical, that is not an option against oppression, is not the option of Jesus; in the long run it leaves the poor at the mercy of the oppressor.

The second element is *partiality*. We insist on this because it has been said, fallaciously, that "equality" (or at least a gentler inequality) is possible, a sufficiently human "universality," and that this miracle would come about through neoliberal globalization. The flaw in the metaphor is that there's room for "everyone" on the globe, which is an obvious lie. We mention this to emphasize that if the goal is salvation for the poor of this world, they must be explicitly placed at the center. This utopia doubtlessly will not be realized, but if we don't even "think" this way, there will be no solution.

We insist on it because even democracy—if we accept its values and minimize its limitations, hypocrisies, even crimes (including those committed by real democratic governments, especially toward the Third World peoples outside their borders, and sometimes within their borders)—does not place the poor at the center of reality, not even at the center of its utopias. Two hundred years ago the idea of human rights applied to the English "freemen," the white men of Virginia, the French bourgeoisie, but not to everyone, not even the people around them: English and French peasants, North American black people and slaves, although in theory they too were considered "human beings." Citizens were at the center. That remains partly true. "Men are unequal even before they are born."[24] That is why a contrary thesis is needed, and a willingness to take sides: "Human rights are the rights of the poor."[25] The Church must not only help the poor, but consciously place them at the center of reality; it is not enough to remember the kindness of the common good. In this sense, the option is doubly partial.

The third element is *engagement*. By this I am not directly referring to ascetical attitudes of impoverishment and closeness to the poor, but to something more metaphysical: an obsession with being "real," in a world of poor people. The Church should seek to be holy, or perfect, or authentic, or evangelical; the term of choice changes over time. I prefer to say "real," that is, it should make the world of the poor its own world. This means, *sub specie contrarii*, that it should not be ashamed to be itself and act itself in a world of poverty.

The example that always occurs to me is scary, but I can't think of a better example of a "real" Church. In Archbishop Romero's words:

> I am glad, brothers and sisters, that our Church is being persecuted precisely because of its option for the poor and because it seeks to be incarnated in the interest of the poor.[26]

> It would be sad, in a nation where people are so horribly murdered, if there were not also priests among the victims. They are the witness of a Church incarnated in the problems of the people.[27]

The words are powerful, even rhetorical, but the idea is clear. There were many things to say about that Church, including about its limitations and sins. But what was beyond doubt is that it was Salvadoran, it was "real." He also saw it as real because of its participation in the positive side of the Salvadoran people: their creativity, generosity, strength, persistence. . . .

The fourth element is *humility*. As much as the nonpoor try to understand the poor, even in order to help them, there is an abyss between them. I have said this repeatedly: humanity is divided between those who cannot take life for granted, the poor, and those who do take it for granted, the nonpoor. Whatever we say about the poor, whatever we think about helping them, must include a strong element of humility, of unknowing. And perhaps this unknowing can be understood as a constitutive element of "knowing" the mystery. It is true of God, and it is true of the poor.

Perhaps in accepting this abyss, the unknowing that it expresses and the humility it requires, we can touch the deepest roots of what is widely accepted today: the right to be different. This is seen in many spheres of reality—gender, culture, religion—but perhaps the fundamental difference is between taking and not taking life for granted. The difference itself is clear. Respecting and honoring it is respecting a right.

We know this is hard to do, not only in hegemonic imperial policies but also in policies of aid and cooperation. In this context the option for the poor must be permeated with humility so that in the end it will not be an option for oneself disguised as an option for the other, the poor; this is true of persons, institutions, even nongovernmental organizations.

In conclusion: We have outlined the fundamental dimensions of the option for the poor in today's world. We have described it in generic but understandable terms: giving the poor life, word, name. All this must clearly be historicized and carried out within a specific framework. Around this option revolves a constellation of theoretical, pastoral, even political praxis. We have emphasized the need to return, repeatedly, to the depth of the poor; otherwise the option is just a passing fancy.

Two more things. First, in our description of the diversity of praxis, of different ways to express the option, the main "tools" are mercy and the word, which are absolutely evangelical realities with great historical potential. Second, although we have not talked about the political dimension of the poor, that is always needed. Perhaps the very fact of carrying out the option, as we have described it, will help to generate a collective consciousness in the poor which will lead them into the political sphere, with its struggles and utopias.

In the next essay we address the most fundamental theme in the option for the poor: letting ourselves be saved by the poor. Here let me anticipate the reason for its importance: it is a benefit for the Church that the poor can move it to conversion.

The Church (and the society) seriously needs to be challenged, for it has a natural tendency to hide its miseries. The challenge is thus a benefit and an element of salvation. *Ecclesia semper reformanda* and *casta meretrix* are usually just words, no matter how often they are repeated in official documents. As a human and sinful institution, the Church can also identify with the words of the cardinal archbishop of Seville in Dostoevski's *The Great Inquisitor*: "Lord, don't return." The historical existence of a reality that challenges the Church and moves it to conversion is thus a great benefit and a step toward salvation.

The Church faces many challenges, but we believe none is more vigorous—and leaves the Church more defenseless—than the poor and the victims of this world.[28] Puebla said rightly that they move the Church to conversion. We might add that if they do not move a heart of stone, it is unlikely that anything can.

Moreover, the poor and the victims strengthen us not only to feel the challenge of conscience, but to be converted. In an old tradition, penitents stand before a crucifix in order to be moved to conversion. Ignacio de Loyola would confront a repentant sinner with the crucified Christ and make him ask, "What shall I do?"—implying the need for generous acts. Ignacio Ellacuría historicized the question in a world of poor people and victims: "Ask, what shall I do to bring down the crucified people from the cross?"[29]

This challenge is usually avoided rather than accepted as a benefit, but it is a salvific benefit of the first order. And if the challenge is accompanied by forgiveness, as often happens when it does not come from other powerful institutions but from the poor and the victims, then we may well feel ourselves to be "sinners," because we can recognize "forgiveness" when it comes from the poor; as Karl Rahner has said, "Only the forgiven one knows he is a sinner." Both things, knowing that we are forgiven and that we are sinners, bring salvation to the Church. And the poor are the principal actors in both cases. If the poor embrace and forgive, then we can fully understand them as the mediation of the heavenly Father who justifies by grace.

And in the last analysis, what is all this for? Why should we make the option for the poor, work for their salvation, look to them for salvation? Years ago I wrote that the poor have "doctrinal authority" to show us the ultimate truth of things.[30] In more radical terms, Metz speaks of their moral authority: "Moral universalism has its roots in the recognition of the authority of those who suffer. . . . The Church too is subject to that obedience. It cannot be ecclesiologically codified, for not even the Church can appeal from the authority of those who suffer—to whom obedience is owed."[31] We must remember that, in order to understand and carry out the option for the poor.

—*Translated by Margaret Wilde*

3

Extra Pauperes Nulla Salus

A Short Utopian-Prophetic Essay

The Need to Reverse the Course of History

In his speech in Barcelona on November 6, 1989, which was programmatic and turned out to be the last speech he gave, Ignacio Ellacuría
said:

> Only with hope and utopian vision can one believe and be motivated
> enough to try, along with all the poor and oppressed people of the
> world, to reverse history, to subvert it and thrust it in another
> direction. . . . What on another occasion I called copro-historical
> analysis, that is, the study of the feces of our civilization, seems to
> reveal that this civilization is gravely ill and that, in order to avoid a
> dreadful and fatal outcome, it is necessary to try to change it from
> within itself.[1]

This gravely ill civilization is the civilization of capital, which Ellacuría
also called the civilization of wealth. It makes "the accumulation of
capital the motor of history and makes its possession and enjoyment the
principle of humanization."[2] It has offered no adequate solution to the
basic wants and needs of the majority of the people on the planet, nor
has it provided them a humane and fraternal civilization. The conclu-

---

In this chapter we gather together ideas, sometimes whole paragraphs, that we have
published over the last few years—more concretely, in the following articles of the journal
Concilium: "Redención de la globalización: Las víctimas," 293 (2001): 129–39; "Revertir
la historia," 308 (2004): 811–20; "La salvación que viene de abajo: Hacia una humanidad
humanizada," 314 (2006): 29-40. And also "La opción por los pobres: dar y recibir,"
Revista Latinoamericana de Teología 69 (2006): 219–61.

sion is clear: "In a world sinfully shaped by the dynamic of capital and wealth, it is necessary to commence a different dynamic, one that can salvifically overcome that other dynamic."[3]

This different dynamic is the one that arises from a civilization of labor, which Ellacuría also called a civilization of poverty. "Deriving from a materialist humanism that has been transformed by the light of Christian inspiration, it makes the universal satisfaction of basic necessities the principle of development and makes the growth of shared solidarity the foundation of humanization."[4]

Ellacuría insisted, obviously, on maintaining all the important achievements of the historical present: scientific research, which has improved many aspects of life; the ethico-cultural progress in human rights; and other ideological-cultural advances, such as certain elements of modern-day democracies. To "overcome" salvifically, then, does not mean "starting from zero," but it does mean "starting all over" and "starting up against" the principles that shape the present civilization of wealth.

For Ellacuría, in his day, the evils that needed to be overcome were evident. They included poverty, expanded exploitation, the scandalous distance between rich and poor, and ecological destruction, as well as the perversion of the advances of democracy, and the ideologization and manipulation of human rights. . . . And he insisted ever more strongly on the deterioration, degeneration, and prostitution of the human spirit, in a word, on the dehumanization of society, about which there was, and is, little real discussion. Suffice it to recall the criticism he spelled out in his Barcelona speech, his criticism of "the palpable dehumanization of those who abandon the task of painstakingly making themselves and prefer the agitated, harried productivism of possessing and accumulating wealth, power, and honor, and the ever-changing gamut of consumer goods."[5] Such is the grave case of dehumanization, ever-present and specific, that is a product of the civilization of capital.

To overcome the present civilization of wealth and its evils, Ellacuría proposes "to awaken a collective consciousness of substantial changes . . . and to create economic, political, and cultural models that make it possible for a civilization of labor to replace a civilization of capital."[6] Both tasks are necessary, but both are also extremely difficult. To achieve them, he urgently encourages his listeners toward a utopian vision and toward hope, together "with all the poor and oppressed people of the world."[7] Thus do we find a proper focus for the subject of this essay: in order to heal a gravely ill civilization there is required, in some form or other, the contribution of the poor and the victims.

A World That Is Gravely Ill

We have recalled Ellacuría's words from 1989. And today? History has, without a doubt, brought about important new developments. René Girard believes that, seen in historical perspective, a new spirit is emerging in humanity, one that is more concerned about victims and more compassionate toward them: "Never before has any society been so concerned with victims as is ours."[8] Girard makes it clear, though, that "it is really only a great comedy"[9] and that in speaking thus he does not wish to "exonerate from all censure the world in which we live."[10] Nevertheless, however, he insists that "the phenomenon is unprecedented";[11] it could be something akin to what happened during the axial age, from the eighth to the sixth centuries B.C.E., of which Jaspers speaks. And Bishop Pedro Casaldáliga, despite the severe condemnation that we cite below, affirms that "humanity 'is moving' and is turning toward truth and justice. There is much idealism and much commitment on this disenchanted planet."[12] However this may be, in our present day we are basically still involved in a civilization of capital, which generates extreme scarcities, dehumanizes persons, and destroys the human family: it produces impoverished and excluded people and divides the world into conquerors and conquered. Our civilization continues to be "gravely ill." In the words of Jean Ziegler, both material life and the life of the spirit "have received death threats."[13]

Evils Suffered by the Majorities: Injustice, Cruelty, and Death

There is more wealth on Earth, but also more injustice. Africa has been called the world's "dungeon," a continental *Shoah*. Some 2.5 billion people survive on Earth on less than two Euros a day, and 25,000 persons die every day of hunger, according to the FAO. Desertification threatens the lives of 1.2 billion people in some one hundred different countries. —Bishop Pedro Casaldáliga[14]

At times one hears that the present globalized world offers new possibilities of life to poor peoples, especially by means of migration. There is no need to exclude that possibility, nor to deny that migration may alleviate some evils, especially when it happens out of dire necessity. However, the migrations today are not a simple readjustment of the human species—something that has occurred often in history and can be potentially enriching. Present-day migrations, because of their causes and the ways they take place, are especially cruel. Let us quote again from Casaldáliga:

> Immigrants are denied simple fraternity, and even the ground beneath their feet. The United States is building a 1,500-kilometer wall against Latin America, while Europe is raising up a barrier against Africa in southern Spain. All of this, besides being iniquitous, is programmed. One African immigrant, in an astonishing letter, written "behind the walls of separation," warns us: "I beseech you not to think that it is normal for us to live this way; it is in fact the result of great injustice that has been established and sustained by inhuman systems that kill and impoverish. . . . Do not support this system with your silence."[15]

With hardly the blink of an eye, we continue on with our madness and our shamelessness, in which injustice, cruelty, contempt, growing inequality, and often cover-up converge. To mention just a few facts:

- The spending on arms is estimated at $2.68 billion a day, and agricultural subsidies in the United States and the European Union are one billion dollars a day. (Federico Mayor Zaragoza)[16]
- The arms market is one of the most profitable for all governments of the international community. The countries of the G-8, together with China, are responsible for 90% of arms exports. At least a half million people are killed annually with small arms. (Amnesty International)[17]
- The objective of globalization is to dominate other people, another country, another world. . . . Globalization is nothing but westernization. The West wants to be the center of the world. (Aminata Traoré)[18]

All of this—whether hunger, the spread of arms, or forced displacement of people for lack of land, water, or soil—results in death, either directly or indirectly. And to these hard realities must be added many others which in one way or another lead to the same end: AIDS, malaria (necessarily involved with the scandal of multinational pharmaceutical firms),[19] unemployment, exclusion, and a long list of others. None of this is part of the order of nature. It is a product of historical causes, and it is important to recognize that in our day and age, the fundamental cause is capitalism:

> "Real capitalism" is responsible for the terrible ethico-moral organization of the world economy and for the shameful, irrational, and

absurd coexistence, in an ever more integrated world, of outrageous poverty with unprecedented wealth.[20]

All this tends to take place today without anyone noticing it.[21] Criticism, when it does exist, is more concerned with what adjective to use ("*savage* capitalism"), instead of treating the topic of capitalism itself and the principle that sustains it: the right of property.[22] As long as that principle is maintained as absolute and untouchable, every economy will be structurally configured by a dynamic of oppression, human beings will be classified according to their ability to produce wealth, their right to possess and enjoy wealth will prolong and even increase human oppression, and most certainly it will widen the distance between the haves and the have-nots.

Ultimately, such a society is a cruel society, because of the suffering that it produces among the oppressed and because of its unfeeling attitude toward the suffering that it generates, even with important exceptions, in a world of abundance. Leonardo Boff states, "When future generations judge our epoch, they will call us barbarous, inhuman, and ruthless because of our enormous insensitivity in the face of the sufferings of our own brothers and sisters."[23] One example: "If there existed even a modicum of humanity and compassion among human beings, the transference of barely 4% of the 225 greatest fortunes in the world would be sufficient to provide food, water, health, and education to the whole of humanity."[24] We are dealing with a metaphysical obscenity.

Such quotes could be endlessly multiplied.[25] They are from today, not from some era of preglobalization, and they are from far-sighted and responsible sources. But if we want such data to help heal "grave illness" of our civilization, we would do well to heed the warning of a Comboni missionary who has spent eighteen years in Uganda: "Statistics don't bleed; people do."

We are always seeking excuses to avoid confronting—or even coming into contact with—reality. Looking into the past, we might say that fifty years ago there was more misery on the planet, and in a sense that is true. But we must tell the whole truth; only then will we confront reality with honesty.[26] Looking into the future, we might even feel euphoric: in two decades China may eliminate the hunger of hundreds of millions of people[27]—though we do not know whether they will achieve that goal and, even if they do, at what human cost.[28]

But even if we try to be optimistic, our reality continues to cry out, "It just can't be this way!"[29] "God is furious."[30] "The irrational has become rational."[31] And we haven't even mentioned Afghanistan, Iraq, Somalia, Darfur. . . .

Evils Affecting the Spirit of Human Beings: Dehumanization

What we have just said means that the vast majority of our world is a "crucified people . . . whose human semblance is continually effaced by the sin of the world, whom the world's powers keep despoiling of everything, and whose life they keep snatching away, their life above all."[32]

In this text Ellacuría insists on the despoilment of life, and with that we begin. The civilization of wealth does not produce life; it produces death in diverse forms, to greater or lesser degrees. Furthermore, it does not humanize, and that is what we want to insist on now. It is already inhuman to deprive others of life, but all the more inhuman when this is done unjustly, cruelly, and contemptuously—even in the name of some god. Furthermore, it is inhuman when the despoilment of some people's lives is closely connected with other people's unrestrained pursuit of success and the good life. The civilization of wealth produces primordial ways of thinking and feeling that in turn mold cultural and ideological structures that contaminate the very air we breathe. Therefore, not only is the *oikos*, the basic symbol of life's reality, gravely ill and in need of salvation, but so is the very air that the spirit breathes. We are dehumanized by going beyond the pale of truth—by concealment of the truth and proliferation of the lie, by silence in the face of scandalous inequality between rich and poor, by the dormant state of the rich—and also of the poor—that is precisely intended and shaped by the mass media.

It is dehumanizing also to go beyond the pale of basic decency, as in the mockery that is made of victims, with complete panache, through the denial of fundamental human rights to whole peoples or through wholesale disregard of important resolutions of the United Nations; as in the widespread corruption in almost all spheres of power, half justified by the unquestioned dogma of profit; as in the impunity that exists before, during, and after the perpetration of atrocities, often committed by governments themselves. And it is also beyond the pale of decency to convert Western-style democracy into absolute dogma, without regard to verification.[33]

It is dehumanizing also to go beyond the pale of maturity, above all in this time when we declare that the world has "come of age." We are speaking of those fundamentalisms—individualism, comfort, or pleasure (so soft in appearance, but with grave consequences)—that are accepted without justification and unquestioningly prized and promoted. We are speaking also of the simplistic and infantile attitudes that may express themselves in very pretentious language, sometimes in the political sphere and very frequently in the religious.

It is dehumanizing that the West is obeisant to empire—*imperium magnum latrocinium*, Augustine used to say—even if such language is no longer so common. This obeisance, in whatever form, makes of the West an accomplice in the empire's economic and military crimes and in its violations of human rights. It accepts as normal the arrogance and dominance of some human beings with respect to others. And it accepts obedience to the empire's directives as necessary, or at least comprehensible, if we want to be assured of a "good living," "success," and "security," or whatever passes for definitive salvific goods.

In sum, we are dehumanized by our selfishness[34] and by our insensitivity before the drama of AIDS, exclusion, discrimination, and poverty's endless misery and cruelty. We are dehumanized by our contempt for the poor, for Native peoples, and even for Mother Earth.

Such dehumanization is assumed with an attitude of impotence and naturalness ("That's the way things are!"), and it is hardly noticeable since, in contrast to the evils that produce physical death or move people toward it, the evils of the spirit are not so obviously calculable. But they are harmful.

There is insistence that poverty must be eliminated—that's positive. But the attempts to eliminate it—even without assessing the results—are dehumanizing.

The first dehumanizing aspect of the attempts to eliminate poverty is the way they effectively bracket people's dignity, as if it were a matter of principle, as if one thing had nothing to do with the other. It is simply accepted that any means is good as long as it alleviates poverty. This way of thinking is not only unethical, but is dehumanizing, for we are not talking about feeding a species of wild animal, but about nourishing human beings.

It is also dehumanizing to accept readily in practice, even if theory may dictate otherwise, the sluggish pace of overcoming poverty and the extended time lapses that countries accept. Seen from the perspective of abundance, the pace may appear relatively human and rapid, but seen from the perspective of poverty—and decency—it is inhumanly slow, and in some cases, as in the sub-Saharan countries, there has actually been regression in the dates that were set for certain goals. The United Nations asserts that the millennium goals are already becoming obsolete and that little or nothing has been done to diminish poverty. "Reducing to one-half the number of people who suffer hunger will be accomplished within 145 years, and not by 2015, as 189 heads of states had determined"[35] as part of the millennium goals.

Furthermore, it is dehumanizing that the so-called generosity gap is growing rather than diminishing. "Aid from the rich countries has diminished by 25% in the last 15 years."[36] During this period the per-capita income of the rich nations rose, while the amount assigned to development decreased. Today, the per-capita aid for sub-Saharan Africa is less than it was in 1990.

Dehumanizing also is the blatant way in which, in the search for solutions, ethics is bracketed. No doubt, to eliminate hunger there is need for strategies, technological know-how, and a good dose of political pragmatism. But ignoring ethics is a serious matter. As a ranking official of the FAO has stated, "Solving the hunger problem today is not basically an economic or political problem; it is an ethical problem." It is also a serious matter for reasons of principle: if to resolve human problems we can dispense with the potential of the ethical, then effectiveness and ethics can definitely be divorced from one another, without harm to what is human. It means the disappearance of the ancient ideal, at least in aspiration, of bringing about a convergence of virtue and happiness. There remains only pragmatism, with a strong potential for brutishness.

Something similar must be said about the language that is frequently used concerning human problems such as hunger: resolving such problems requires political will. What needs to be recognized first is that there is no such will, for such hunger still exists. Second, since political will is nothing more than human will, it seems that an effort is being made in the political realm to hide something behind language. If there is no political will, then there is simply no effective human will to eliminate hunger. In the face of the scandal of a hungry world, the language of "political" will appears more respectable. Recourse is made to such language because it conceals far more than the alternative. To speak of "human will" raises the question of whether we human beings really have the will to eliminate hunger. Regarding the political aspect of that will, there can be many debates and evasions, and for that reason such language is preferred. Regarding the human aspect of the will to eliminate hunger, there can be no evasions.

Jean Ziegler states, "A child who dies of hunger dies a murder victim,"[37] words that bring to mind Ivan Karamazov.[38] Recall Ivan's indignation when children were destroyed by dogs on orders of a landlord who was a former military official, and how he refused to be consoled when told that those children would go to a place where they would be embraced in a universal harmony: "If they invite me to that heaven, from this moment, I refuse the invitation."

The ambiguous and obscure language of "globalization" is dehumanizing.

Language can be a source of dehumanization when it is used as a means of manipulation, concealment, and deceit. For that reason, the choice to use one kind of language or another is anything but innocent. Consequently, a battle is always being waged in that regard, so that language comes to signify that which favors determined interests, independently of whether reality is well reflected in it or not. That happens with terms like "democracy" and "liberty," and it used to happen with terms like "socialism" and "revolution." The same happens with religious language, starting with the word "God." Whoever wins the language battle has won half the war—and has gained significant power.

Something of that sort is happening, I believe, with the term "globalization." Something new has happened in history, but to express what that is we do not use terms like "planetization" or "a more bonded, interdependent humanity." The term that has been chosen is "globalization," and I do not believe the choice is completely haphazard. The use of that very term suggests, at least subliminally, that "something good" has happened, and certainly "globalization" sounds better and more humane than "capitalism." The term suggests the idea of salvation, even though a great many of globalization's fruits are evil and at times perverse.

With the word "globalization" an attempt is made to communicate and impose a judgment value: what is happening is good; we live in an inclusive world, one belonging to all, and it is—or soon will be—a basically homogeneous and harmonious world for everybody. We do not live, after all, in an irregular, deformed polyhedron, though it might be possible to fit everybody just as well into such a shape; rather, we live in a world that is on the way to perfection. These statements represent the connotations of "globalization": the beauty of roundness, and the equity that reigns within the whole, the equidistance between all the points on the globe and its center;[39] that globalized world is preached as an eschatological good news, as that for which all humankind has longingly awaited; and nowadays such a world is preached with better arguments—and greater possibilities—than those put forward by Fukuyama

with his "end of history." Concerning all this I would like to make three
critical comments.

The first is that when we use the term "globalization" today, we commit a sin of omission, as if there had not been important globalizations
previously. I mention just two of them, described years ago by
Hinkelammert. First, the "discovery" of America globalized geography
and significantly broadened the self-understanding of human beings,
especially regarding the unity of the human race. Second, the atomic
bomb dropped on Hiroshima in 1945 also globalized the human species, but in a very different way, now because of global fear: the possibility for the first time that the whole of the species could perish. Both
events made possible the discovery and the appreciation of the global
dimensions of the earth and the human family, while at the same time
manifesting the ambiguity that is inherent in all created reality. Nowadays, though, language does not reflect seriously the ambiguity of globalization: whether it consists in planetization or conquest,[40] whether it
has more of one aspect than the other, and which of the two it contains
more. Nor does our language reflect the fears, in the form of impotency
or inevitability, that can be generated by a globalized world: fear of
being absorbed and so losing cultural identity, fear that jobs will be
transferred to other places for the sake of higher profits, fear that new
superpowers will arise. . . .

My second criticism refers to our taking for granted that globalization is automatically a form of progress, so that it is thereby completely
justified and should be promoted without questioning. In reality, Western officialdom is not in the habit of evaluating with honesty the past
history of its own progress, nor does it analyze critically what it today
considers progress. A candid look at the past will make us lose our
innocence. Jürgen Moltmann writes:

> The fields of history's corpses, which we have seen, prohibit us from
> having . . . any ideology of progress and *any taste for globaliza-*
> *tion.* . . . If the achievements of science and technology can be used for
> the annihilation of humanity (and if they *can*, they some day will be),
> it becomes difficult to get enthusiastic about the internet or about
> genetic technology.[41]

The "anti-globalization" or "alternative globalization" movements do
not want, strictly speaking, "more progress," but precisely "another"
world.

A third criticism, in my opinion the most serious, is that language usually conceals what actually gave rise to the term "globalization" and what keeps making it specifically what it is. Economist Luis de Sebastián says that globalization is simply "the present situation of the world economy."[42] It is today's "real capitalism."[43] And with clairvoyance he adds, "Globalization, like every process of social change, has produced winners and losers, beneficiaries and victims."[44] When globalization is seen as economic reality, we learn two important things. As regards its salvific potential, despite its being "global," globalization is no different from other economic processes; it is not as if, by its nature, it only produces good things. Globalization also produces evils, losers, victims. As regards its evaluation, this will vary, depending on whether this is conducted among the winners or among the losers.

In a world of poverty, conspicuous abundance and silence in the face of misery are both dehumanizing. And more dehumanizing still is the simultaneity of the two phenomena. We look at some recent examples.

Singapore, July 6, 2005. That day there was a celebration of the city's selection as the site of the 2012 Olympic Games, with all the pretensions of universality that this implies. However, the planetary dimension of the Games did little to promote a greater awareness of the universal reality of the planet and its diverse peoples and cultures, and even less did it help shed light on the oppression and domination of some people at the hands of others and of the many aberrant conflicts and wars. The reality of the planet was thoroughly diluted in the language of pomp and ended up being distorted by deceitful and hypocritical language.

There is celebration of the apotheosis of sports, though properly speaking it is not really sports, but elitist sports that are celebrated, that which has sold its identity to industry and commerce. There is celebration of liturgies, of Olympic Games, of world championships, that ever more resembles a Hollywood production, the fashion industry, or even the world of pulp fiction. The real center of it all is Wall Street. In view of the misery that plagues the countries south of the Sahara, the money that moves among the elite of European soccer and U.S. basketball is shameless.

The image left by Singapore is one of pomp, wastefulness, and worship of prosperity. It entertains and energizes, but at the deepest level it narcotizes. Symbolically, it projects the whole of the planet on a screen, but what it thinks least about is the 6 billion human beings who inhabit the planet—and the vast number of those who barely survive.

Gleneagles, England, G-8, July 8, 2005. On that day, the powerful ones presented themselves, though with a certain semblance of humility, as benefactors of humanity: they forgave the debt of some African countries. But Aminata Traoré told them the truth: "We are accustomed to G-8 announcements that in the end are never made effective. . . . Because of their free-market policies, what they will do is negotiate away the competitiveness of our economies in relation to the markets of the North."[45]

The injustice is manifest, but what we would like to insist on now is its conspicuous character. In seven capitals of the world the G-8 promoted Live 8 concerts in a campaign to collect funds and develop awareness of and solidarity with Africa. But there was no real generosity. The greatest beneficiaries of the concerts have been Time-Warner, Ford Motor Company, Nokia, and EMI Music. Once again, industry takes priority over music, and the North is enriched through Africa's pain.

Alongside this ostentation in the North is the silence about the South. Just one example from recent days. The organization Doctors without Borders published a list of "the most forgotten humanitarian crises in the international media during 2005." They take for granted the existence of innumerable crises and therefore concentrate only on the "most painful and shameful," the "humanitarian" crises. And since they take for granted that all crises are usually forgotten, they ask about the "most forgotten" ones. Heading the list is still the Democratic Republic of the Congo: "Millions of persons subjected to a situation of extreme destitution and daily violence that has gotten worse in recent months; nonetheless, they are completely off the radar of the rest of the world."[46] That is silence in the face of the reality of the Third World.

Besides this we find the everyday cases of forgetfulness, which are now just second nature. The event of 9/11 is well known: terrorism against the United States. But 10/7 is completely unknown: it was October 7, 2001, the day when the international democratic community bombed Afghanistan. A date well known in Spain is 3/11, when there was an attack in Madrid (March 11, 2004). But on March 20, 2003, the bombing of Iraq began, and 3/20 does not exist. The poor have no calendar. They have no existence. Forgetfulness is natural. And all this occurs in a world that is more interrelated than ever before, a globalized world.

The extraordinary and growing inequality between the poor and the rich is dehumanizing.

Finally, we find dehumanizing the insensitivity involved in the very fact that the rich live cheek by jowl with the poor, which appalls us even before asking whether any causal relationship exists between the wealth of the former and the misery of the latter. We see a profound inequality of wealth and opportunity that has become something normal, something that we believe belongs to the order of nature, not to that of history.

The parable of the Rich Man and the Poor Lazarus is the true parable of our world. The story apparently had its origin in an Egyptian legend recalled either by Jesus or by Luke; such an origin means that the scandal comes from afar and persists throughout history. For me the most impressive part of the parable is Abraham's final statement to the rich man: "They will not be convinced, even if someone should arise from the dead" (Luke 16:31). And it is true. We have no idea what needs to be done before the "international community" begins to feel remorse about this extraordinary inequality of opportunity between rich and poor and begins to respond with radical compassion.

Even before we ask why it is happening, our simple contemplation of the cheek-by-jowl coexistence of the rich man and Lazarus, who represents all humanity, should cause us to be ashamed. It is not simply unjust, but disgraceful, that in the world of abundance four hundred times more in the way of resources is spent to care for the gestation and birth of a baby than in Ethiopia; that a Salvadoran woman in a sweat-shop earns twenty-nine cents for each shirt that the multinational Nike sells to the NBA for forty-five dollars; that "in terms of broadcast information, one kidnapped white person continues to be worth more than a thousand tortured and murdered Congolese";[47] that the abyss between rich and poor is growing rapidly, according to the United Nations Development Program: the disproportion has increased from 30 to 1 in 1960, to 60 to 1 in 1990, and to 74 to 1 in 1997. And nobody reacts. Eduardo Galeano says that "a U.S. citizen is worth as much as fifty Haitians." And he wonders: "What would happen if one Haitian were worth as much as fifty U.S. citizens?"

On February 13, 2001, a soccer game was played between the teams Real Madrid and Lazio; the market value of just the twenty-two starting players would have been about $700 million, as sportswriters reported before the game with no sense of indignation, but rather with satisfaction. They did not report, however, that that figure might well have equaled a major proportion of a black African nation's annual budget, and was perhaps twice as large as Chad's whole budget. And according to what one hears these days, I doubt that things have improved much since then.

The civilization of wealth gives rise to many of these evils. Afterward it covers them up. Furthermore, it dehumanizes. It makes the human spirit breathe a poisoned air. At times strong words are heard, such as those we have cited, and there are also others. John Paul II: "Today, more than yesterday, the *war* of the powerful against the weak has opened up profound divisions between the rich and the poor."[48] Mayor Zaragoza: "The most powerful and prosperous countries have abdicated democratic principles (justice, liberty, equality, solidarity) in favor of the laws of the market."[49] Harold Pinter: "Without a firm determination . . . to define the authentic truth of our lives and our societies, . . . we have no hope of restoring what we have almost completely lost—our dignity as persons."[50] J. Taubes: "We are debtors, and we have little time left to pay off our debts."[51] And though it may cut to the quick, there is still much truth in what Ellacuría said about the United States: it mocks democracy and its principles. "It does not respect the will of the majority of humankind or the sovereignty of other nations, nor does it respect the United Nations resolutions that are approved with massive majorities or the sentences of the international court of the Hague."[52] (Today he would denounce the savagery of preventive warfare and its theoretical justification, as well as the atrocity of using the term "collateral damage" for what are in fact monstrous murders.) All this continues to sink into oblivion and silence. The democracies do not make opposing such lies a central concern. And very few of the churches dare to take their prophetic duty seriously.

There are always a Romero and a Casaldáliga, a Chomsky and a Galeano, as before there were an Adorno and a Martin Luther King. But there are not many. Nor are there many like Ivan Karamazov, ready to refuse entrance into the paradise of this industrial, globalized, and democratic world of ours, which produces—or tolerates—the death of children. And the most radical dehumanization of all is to keep living normally in this world *etsi paupers non darentur*, to give a twist to Bonhoeffer's phrase *etsi Deus non daretur*.

The Poor and Salvation

The Need for a New Logic to Understand Salvation

Paul exclaimed, "Wretched man that I am! Who will deliver me from this body of death?" (Rom. 7:24). Our times have little room for that type of question, but the terror caused by the world we have described above prompts a similar question: "Who will deliver us from this cruel and inhuman world?"

In the face of such an immense problem, our response must obviously be modest, but we can attempt to offer at least the beginning of an answer. We will do so by understanding salvation in relation to the poor and by seeing in the poor a locus and a potential for salvation. Although it may sound defiant, the formulation *extra pauperes nulla salus* is indeed quite modest. Strictly speaking, we are not saying that with the poor there is automatic salvation; we claim only that without them there is no salvation—although we do presuppose that in the poor there is always "something" of salvation. What we aim to do, ultimately, is to offer hope, in spite of everything. *From the world of the poor and the victims can come salvation for a gravely ill civilization.*

Our way of proceeding will be fundamentally through mystagogy, that is, by trying to enter into a mystery that exceeds our grasp. Even the full knowledge of what a human being is exceeds our grasp, and therefore so also does the full knowledge of what salvation is—although some of its elements are not at all mysterious, such as the eradication of hunger. That very formula exceeds our grasp: *extra pauperes nulla salus*. Of course, concepts and arguments are necessary for entering into the mystery, but they do not suffice. We must also take into account—and make converge with those concepts and arguments—wisdom, reflection, testimony, and experience, and certainly in this case we need the *esprit de finesse* of which Pascal speaks.

The formula defies instrumental reason, and our hubris rebels against it. For that reason it does not appear, as far as I know, in any modern or postmodern texts, for it is not easy to accept that salvation comes from the unenlightened.[53] What prevails is the metaphysical axiom: whether saved or damned, "Reality is us!"

The formula is also a limit statement and therefore acquires meaning only after an analysis of the different contributions of the poor to salvation. And most definitely it is a negative formulation, which does not make it any less, but rather more, important: indeed, it seems to us that the more important things are these days, the more they need to be formulated in negative terms.[54] But even with all these difficulties, we maintain the formula, for it is an expression that is vigorous and is suitable for breaking—at least conceptually—the logic of the civilization of wealth.

Accepting the formula presents still other difficulties. For some people, the greatest difficulty is the inability of poor people to produce goods on a massive scale. For me personally, the major difficulty lies in the fact that even the world of the poor is invaded with the *mysterium iniquitatis*. There come to mind the evils we see daily among the poor, and we are reminded of this wickedness by those who live and work directly with

them. In one way or another they ask us if we are not idealizing the poor
or yielding to "the myth of the noble savage," a phrase I heard in Spain
during the quincentennial celebration in 1992. And it is not easy to give
an answer that soothes the spirit. Seeing the poor in their base communities is one thing: generous and committed to liberation, both their
own and others', under the inspiration of Archbishop Romero; it is another thing to see them disenchanted, spoiled by the world of abundance and its offerings, struggling against one another to survive. Then
there are the horrors of the Great Lakes region of Africa, or the dozen
daily murders in El Salvador. All of these horrors happen in places where
poor people live, even though the immediate responsibility is not only,
nor always, theirs. We do not even think that the principal responsibility is theirs. And we must also take into account that poor people's
reality varies greatly with different times and places.

The theological novelty of this formula also presents difficulties. Some
type of relation has always existed between the poor and Christian faith,
as we can see in various ways.

1. Our faith allows the poor to move us to extreme indignation, to limitless compassion, and even to radical conversion, which can lead to
   the "option for the poor" (Medellín) and to living in obedience to
   "the authority of those who suffer" (J. B. Metz).
2. An ultimate question is raised about whether and why we believe in
   God (theodicy), when it seems that God cannot or will not eliminate
   the horrors of our world.
3. Our salvation or damnation depends on our attitude with respect to
   the poor: "Come, blessed of my Father, because I was hungry and
   you gave me food. . . . Depart from me, you cursed . . ." (Matt. 25).
4. Finally, since as believers we are "sacraments" of God—representing
   either God's "presence" or "absence," depending on how we act toward the poor—one way or the other, we will be able to understand
   what the Scriptures denounce when they repeat five times (three referring to God and two to Christ) that "because of you my name is
   despised among the nations" (Isa. 52:5, Septuagint version; Ezek.
   36:20–22; Rom. 2:24; James 2:7; 2 Pet. 2:2). Or we will make real
   what Jesus asks of us: "Let your light so shine before men, that they
   may see your good works and give glory to your Father who is in
   heaven" (Matt. 5:16).

Medellín gave special importance to the "option for the poor," but
we now go a step further, and do so with some novelty: we propose "the

option to let salvation come from the poor." Accepting such a proposal is not easy; a new logic is needed. We do not simply add a new concept to an already established mode of thinking. Rather, the new logic is the product of a basic globalizing attitude, with a constitutive caesura: not only is it necessary to be and to act on behalf of the poor (Kant's question, what must I *do*?), but we must also pose the other two Kantian questions: what can I *know*? and what can I *hope for*? We would add two further questions: what can I *celebrate*? and what can I *receive*? And all of this "from among the poor." If in answering these questions poor people become a central theme, then the mode of thinking can be moved by a new and different logic, and we will find reasonable the acceptance and the understanding of the formula *extra pauperes nulla salus*. It is not at all easy, but however that may be, the added dimension of the new logic is necessary.

Such a new way of thinking is what we are trying to offer in this modest essay. In so doing, we are guided by the poetic/creative/prophetic intuition of Bishop Pedro Casaldáliga and by the analytic intuition of Ignacio Ellacuría. The reader will also become aware of how much our thought must wrestle with complexity and uncertainty in treating this topic. The urge to engage in the struggle comes from Rahner's statement, "It just can't be that way!" and from some words of Casaldáliga, who was kind enough to write me: "You say it well, and it needs to be repeated incessantly: outside the poor there is no salvation, outside the poor there is no Church, outside the poor there is no Gospel." And of course we have the hope that others will correct, develop, and complement what we are going to say.

The New Logic of Experience

It happens very often that visitors who arrive from places of abundance find among the poor and the victims a certain "something" that is new and unexpected. That happens when the visitors discover in the world of the poor "something" that is good and positive. They have found "salvation." From Brazil José Comblin writes:

The mass media speak of the poor always in negative terms, as those who don't have property, those who don't have culture, those who have nothing to eat. Seen from outside, the world of the poor is pure negativity. Seen from within, however, the world of the poor has vitality; they struggle to survive, they invent an informal economy and they build a different civilization, one of solidarity among people who recognize each other as equals—a civilization with its own forms of expression, including art and poetry.[55]

These words affirm that in the world of the poor there are important values; further, they build a civilization of solidarity. This is not an isolated opinion—it is repeated often by others. Many people today seek a more human humanity, and we say this without redundancy, just as Luther was seeking a benevolent God. But people do not find such humanity in the societies of abundance, or in globalization, or even in the democratic order. People do find important elements of humanity in the world of the poor: joy, creativity, patience, art and culture, hope, solidarity. This experience is dialectical, for they have found human life on the "reverse side of the world of the rich." Such experience is salvific, for it generates hope for a more human world. And it is an experience of grace, for it arises where we least expect it.

Chilean theologian Ronaldo Muñoz says something similar in response to the optimistic report of the United Nations Development Program for 2005. He tempers our enthusiasm for the report and recalls the serious ills that still afflict the majority of people. But he insists above all on seeing things in a different way, from a different perspective:

Rather, we should be amazed at the forbearance and the personal and social development of the women; amazed at the spontaneous solidarity of so many poor people toward their more needy neighbors and companions; amazed at the new organizations of adults and young people, who keep rising up against wind and tide to share in life, to work and celebrate together; amazed at the new dignity of the Mapuche people and their struggle for their rights; amazed at the small Christian communities, Catholic and Evangelical, that keep cropping up and yielding fruits of harmony and hope.[56]

From India, Felix Wilfred, having witnessed what happened during the tsunami, describes both the positive and the negative sides of the world of the poor. And he concludes:

Facing up to human suffering and responding to it in terms of compassion has developed in the victims some of the values we need in order to support a different sort of world: solidarity, humanity, a spirit of sharing, survival techniques, readiness to assume risks, resistance, and firm determination in the midst of adversities. In the world of the victims, as opposed to the world of empire and globalization, the good is not identified with "success." The good and the just are ideals that the world needs in order to struggle unremittingly to attain something. The cultural resources of the poor, which reflect the values and ideals of a world of the future, help them to confront life with both individual and collective courage.[57]

Let these quotes suffice. Obviously we cannot deduce from them a thesis, but they do express something fundamental: there is "something" to be discovered in the world of the poor. These people, who do not take life for granted (as we, who are not poor, so often do), these people who die before their time, who have (almost) all the powers of the world against them, still possess "something" that makes them truly live and that they offer to others. That "something" consists of human goods, more than material, and it is therefore "something" humanizing. Those goods are the ones that are not found, or are found only with greater difficulty, in the world of those who are not poor.

The "poor," with all the variety of shades that we will analyze, and above all the "poor with spirit," as Ellacuría called them (thus systematically unifying the beatitudes of Luke and Matthew[58]), are those who humanize and offer salvation, those who can offer inspiration and energy for the creation of a civilization based on solidarity, as opposed to selfishness. For this reason Ellacuría used to speak of "the immense spiritual and human wealth of the poor and of Third World peoples."[59] How many of *those kind* of poor people there are in reality will vary, according to times and places. Obviously not all are like that. In the world of the poor, goodness and evil frequently coexist, especially in times of great crisis. But as regards the healing of a gravely ill society, I believe there are "more than enough" of them. The problem is to take them into account.

Most important of all, in the world of the poor a logic is generated that allows reality to be seen in a different way. Such a logic makes it plain that salvation cannot be identified simply with progress and development—an insight we consider significant. Such a logic makes it plain that salvation comes from the poor. Thus, the experience of grace is for the nonpoor. The option for the poor is not just a matter of *giving to* them, but of *receiving from* them.

The Logic of Salvation in the Christian and Biblical Tradition

What we have just said should come as a total surprise, though it needs some explanation. The nucleus of the logic described is already present—in idealized form—in the biblical tradition concerning Jesus of Nazareth, even though it is ignored by Western culture. The content of salvation fully appears in that tradition, both in symbolic form and in several other dimensions, such as the historical/social dimension of the *reign of God*, the personal dimension of the *heart of flesh,* and the transcendent dimension of the *new heaven.* These dimensions do not offer concrete models or recipes for salvation, but we can find in them basic elements that show us how salvation is produced and expressed.

For that tradition it is fundamental that salvation comes from the world of the poor, and that it spreads out from there into diverse realms. In the Old Testament Yahweh's option on behalf of a poor, oppressed people is quite evident. We also see, at important junctures of history, that the symbolic bearers of salvation are the small and the weak, and above all—mysteriously—the victims, the servant in his or her individual and collective dimension. Conversely, from the upper strata of society, from the realm of power and abundance, no salvation comes. In fact, the Deuteronomic tradition makes the kings—symbols of power—look pretty bad, with only two exceptions: Josiah and Hezekiah.

From that same perspective are also presented Jesus and the salvation that he brings. Regarding Jesus himself, the savior *par excellence*, there is historically an insistence on his smallness: people say, "We do not know where this fellow comes from" (John 6:14), because he comes from Nazareth, a small and insignificant village from which nothing good can ever come. And transcendentally it is claimed that he became *sarx*, flesh, and assumed the weakness of flesh (John 1:14). But I would like to insist on something that is usually neglected. We ask ourselves where salvation came from for Jesus himself, in his historical form; we ask if something of that salvation came to him also from the world of the poor. I do not know whether, or to what extent, that can be proved from the Gospels, but the matter seems crucial to me. This question should not scandalize us, for it is said also of Jesus, for example, that he went before God with joy and with doubts. As the letter to the Hebrews states, he was like us in all things except sin (Heb. 4:15). He was the firstborn, the eldest brother in the faith (Heb. 12:2).

For that reason we ask not only whether Jesus was salvation for others, but also whether there are indications that others, certainly the heavenly Father and the poor of the earth, were salvation and good news for him. Some indications of that might be in his words: "I give you thanks, Father, for the simple folk have understood and not the wise" (Matt. 11:25). In saying this, was Jesus just overjoyed, or did he feel himself, besides, being evangelized by those simple folk?

We can wonder what Jesus was feeling about the faith of the little ones when he said to the woman with a flow of blood and to the blind Bartimeus (Mark 5:34; 11:52), "Your faith has cured you," and to the sinful woman in the house of Simon the Pharisee, "Go in peace, your faith has saved you" (Luke 7:50); or what he felt when he saw a poor widow throw a few cents into the temple treasury, giving more than the rest, since she was giving all that she had to live on (Mark 12:44); or what he felt before the Canaanite woman, who assured Jesus he was right, "It is true, sir," but who also corrected him movingly, "But it is also true that the dogs eat of the crumbs that the children toss to them." And Jesus declared, "Great is your faith" (Mark 15:28). Without any need to fantasize, we may ask ourselves whether Jesus felt blessed by the faith of these simple folk, whether he would not say within himself—as did Archbishop Romero—"With these people it is not hard to be a good pastor." Our question, then, is whether Jesus experienced salvation coming from the poor.

The most important element for understanding the logic of salvation in this biblical tradition of Jesus of Nazareth is the theologal grounding. The Most High, in order to be the God of salvation, has come down to our history, and he has done so in a twofold manner: he has come down to the human level and, within the human, to what is humanly weak. To express it more precisely, *transcendence* has become *trans-descendence*, benevolent closeness, and thus has become *con-descendence*, affectionate embrace. The same is expressed in the Christological language of the first centuries: *salus autem quoniam caro*. Christ is salvation because he is flesh, *sarx*. That is the new logic.

In principle, grasping that logic is possible anywhere, but it does not normally occur outside the world of the poor. As corroborating evidence, allow me to include some quotes from Jesuits of the Third World; I explain why later. They know well the complexity of salvation. They speak of it in different contexts, but they coincide in their fundamental insight.

From Sri Lanka, Aloysius Pieris writes that the poor are chosen for a salvific mission, not because they are holy but because they are powerless and rejected: "The poor are called to be mediators of salvation for the rich, and the weak are called to liberate the strong."[60] Engelbert Mveng speaks from the context of Cameroon: "The Church of Africa . . . announces the good news of liberation to those who have succumbed to the temptation of power, wealth, and domination."[61] From El Salvador, we have already heard the proposal of Ignacio Ellacuría: the civilization of poverty is necessary in order to overcome and redeem the evils generated by the civilization of wealth.[62] And from Venezuela, Pedro Trigo writes:

> Against the current position, which holds that the salvation of the poor (some of them) will come about only as an overflow or a redundancy of the health of the economic system, the mission of Jesus (and therefore the Christian mission) proclaims that the salvation of the non-poor will come about only through participation in the salvation of the poor. Nowadays that sounds ridiculous.[63]

The reason for quoting Jesuits in this context is that they may well be influenced by the meditation on the two standards in the *Spiritual Exercises* (nos. 136–48) of St. Ignatius. That meditation presents two "principles" of reality that are dynamic, distinct, and counterpoised. One of them leads to humility and thus to all the virtues; the other leads to pride and so to all the vices. To use our terms, one leads to salvation, and the other to damnation. St. Ignatius also insists that what each principle generates, through successive steps of a process, is in a dialectical relationship with what the other generates: insults versus worldly honors, humility versus pride, all the virtues against all the vices. Most important of all is understanding the origin of the whole process: on the one hand it is poverty, which leads to all the virtues and to salvation; on the other it is wealth, which leads to all the vices and to damnation. There is no reason that this Ignatian intuition should be limited to the path of individual perfection; it can also be historicized. Ellacuría thought that "it is a question . . . of awakening dynamics that will structure a new world."[64] By starting from (the civilization of) poverty and opposing (the civilization of) wealth, the world can be turned around.

We already stated that this thesis is countercultural, as it was in Bonhoeffer's day: "Only a God who suffers can save us." It is also difficult to defend, for nonsalvation, the *mysterium iniquitatis*, runs wild in the world of the poor. And the biblical basis for supporting the thesis—"the suffering servant brings salvation"—is the supreme scandal for human reason. But the thesis is necessary, for the world of abundance left to itself does not save, does not produce life for all and does not humanize.

What Salvation and What Poor People

We have argued that in the world of the poor there is "something" salvific that is not easily found in other worlds, as we shall explain in short order. First, however, it should be understood what we mean by the terms "salvation" and the "poor."

Forms of Salvation

The salvation of human beings and the need for it can be seen in different spheres of reality. There is *personal* salvation and *social* salvation, there is *historical* salvation and *transcendent* salvation, although we cannot always neatly distinguish these different types. Here we will concentrate on the historical/social salvation of a gravely ill society. We should also distinguish between salvation as a positive state of affairs and salvation as the process by which that state is reached. In both cases salvation is dialectical, and at times it is dual. It takes place in opposition to other realities and processes, and even in conflict with them.

As a state of affairs, salvation occurs in diverse forms. Letting ourselves be guided *sub specie contrarii* by the negation of life and the dehumanization that we have analyzed, we may say the following: salvation is *life* (satisfaction of basic vital needs), over against poverty, infirmity, and death; salvation is *dignity* (respect for persons and their rights), over against disregard and disdain; salvation is *freedom*, over against oppression; salvation is *fraternity* among human beings who are brought together as *family*, a conception opposed to the Darwinist understanding of the human race as mere *species*; salvation is *pure air*, which the spirit can breathe in order to move toward that which humanizes (honesty, compassion, solidarity, some form of openness to transcendence), over against that which dehumanizes (selfishness, cruelty, individualism, arrogance, crude positivism).

Salvation is concrete—as is seen in the diverse salvations in the Synoptic Gospels. This concreteness should be recalled in order to counter the danger of "universalizing" in nonhistorical ways the concept of salvation and of the realities that accompany it either positively or negatively, such as poverty or development. That is the way the UNDP understands human welfare, and it has its advantages, but obviously the substance of salvation will be understood differently in different places; one understanding will pertain in the residential suburbs of Paris and the World Bank reports, and perhaps quite another in the refugee camps of the Great Lakes district or in the testimonies of the grassroots communities. From Brazil, Bishop Pedro Casaldáliga wrote that "freedom without justice is like a flower on a corpse." "Freedom" and "justice" are both expressions of salvation, but we must not assume that we, from some supposedly universal space, can understand them adequately and prioritize their need and their urgency.

This leads to the question about the locus from which we theorize about salvation. Such theorizing is a very important task today, since globalization, as ideology, seeks to make people believe that the world's

reality is essentially homogeneous and that it is therefore quite unnecessary to ask about the "most appropriate" place for knowing what salvation is or for asking questions about the meaning of being human, or
of hope, or of sin, or of God. Liberation theology does not proceed thus;
it considers extremely important the determination of the locus that is
appropriate for helping us to know the truth about things. That locus is
the world of the poor. For that very reason, liberation theology, and not
other theologies, has been able to formulate, even if negatively, the locus of salvation: *extra pauperes nulla salus.*

Finally, we must also take into account the diverse forms that the
process of salvation takes. Since this process normally takes place against
structures of oppression, salvation often takes the form of liberation:
"It is necessary to liberate from . . ." In addition, there is frequently the
need not only to struggle against the negative products generated by the
structures, but also to yank out their roots; then salvation becomes redemption. For that to happen, according to the Christian biblical tradition, it is necessary to take on the reality of the sin. Thus, inherent in
redemption is the struggle against evil, not only from without, but also
from within, by taking it on.

Diverse Dimensions of the Reality of Poor People

We need also to determine the diverse dimensions of being poor, for the
contribution of poverty to salvation depends on the way it is lived out.[65]

Before classifying the different ways of living poverty, we should recall the basic distinction that Puebla makes when it treats the
soteriological dimension of poor people. First of all, poor people, just
by what they are, independently of "their moral or personal situation,"[66]
"constantly summon [the Church] and call it to conversion"—and such
calling to conversion is a great good. Second, the poor evangelize, they
save, "since many of them practice in their lives the evangelical values
of solidarity, service, simplicity, and readiness to receive the gift of God"
(no. 1147), which is the spirit with which they live their poverty. Let us
now see who the poor people are.

First, there are the *materially* poor, those who do not take life for
granted, those for whom staying alive is their primary task, those for
whom the nearness of death, physical or some other type—of their dignity, of their culture—is their normal fate. This is the economic understanding of being poor, the primordial sense, in which the *oikos*, the
minimal nucleus of life, is threatened. The poor are "those who die
before their time."

Second, there are the *dialectically* poor: not those who are needy simply because nature yields no more, but those who have been impoverished and oppressed. We are speaking of those who are deprived of the fruit of their own labor and who are increasingly excluded from even the opportunity to work. They are likewise deprived of social and political power by the people who, through such plunder, have enriched themselves and have assumed power. This is the sociological understanding of being poor: it denies that the poor can be "associates" or "companions." Besides, they are generally ignored and despised. They are considered nonexistent. They have no name, either in life or in death.

Third, there are the *consciously* poor, those who have achieved an awareness, individual and collective, about the very reality of material poverty and its causes. They have awoken from the dogmatic slumber into which they had been induced; that is, they have stopped believing that their poverty is natural and inevitable—at times, even desired by God.

Fourth, there are the *liberatively* poor, that is, those who transform that new consciousness into grassroots organization and the practice of liberating solidarity. They have become aware of what they themselves can accomplish and their responsibility toward all poor people. They emerge from their own groups and communities to free others.

Fifth, there are the *spiritually* poor, understanding the "spiritually poor" here in a precise sense: those who experience their materiality, their consciousness, and their activity with gratuity, with hope, with mercy, with fortitude in persecution, with love, and even with that greatest love, which is giving one's life for the liberation of the poor majorities (this is the spirit of the beatitudes for living reality fully). Moreover they live thus with trust in and availability to a Father-God, both at the same time: they confide and rest in a Father, and they are completely available to a God who does not let them rest (the spirit of Jesus before the mystery of God). These are the poor with spirit.

Finally, if we view the reality of the poor from the Christian faith perspective, their poverty possesses both a theologal dimension (God's predilection for them) and a Christological dimension (Christ's presence in them). And this—at least to the extent that believers view the poor this way—renders even more radical the appeal of the poor and their offer of salvation to the nonpoor.

The different dimensions of the reality of poor people—depending on epochs and places—will produce diverse types of fruits of salvation. To put it in synthetic form, by their raw reality they can produce conversion and compassion, and also truth and just practice; and by their multiform spirit they can humanize in various ways the impure air that the spirit breathes.

Historical Forms of Salvation Coming from the World of the Poor

It is not easy to characterize the salvation that comes from the world of the poor. To do so we might be helped by thinking of it in three forms: as an opportunity for overcoming dehumanization, as positive elements for humanizing and attaining goods, and as an invitation to universal solidarity.

Overcoming Dehumanization

We have already said it. By virtue of what they are, poor people can move others to conversion, and if *they* do not do so, one may well ask what ever will. Perhaps this point is what is most directly stressed in the phrase *"extra" pauperes*: apart from the poor there is no easy conversion. The nonpoor can see the immense sufferings of the poor and the world's cruelty toward them. They can compare their own "good life" with the life of the poor, above all if they consider their own situation as a kind of "manifest destiny," and they are able to recognize their sin. None of this is easy, and it does not occur on a massive scale, but the opportunity is always there.

Society may boast of having moved beyond concepts like conversion, but such a belief is a serious error. Other concepts, such as change and desiring a different world do not express the radicality of the shift of direction and way of proceeding that is necessary—and even less do they express the necessary pain, repentance, and purpose of amendment, all of which are implied in conversion. Looked at positively, conversion can lead to truth, to hope, and to praxis. Human beings may find there answers to their most basic questions.

What I can know. The poor are *bearers of truth*. By virtue of what they are, they offer light to the world of abundance, so that this world might see its own truth and thus be able to move toward all truth. Ellacuría used to explain this by using two vigorous metaphors, the inverted mirror and feces analysis. A crucified people is like an inverted mirror in which the First World, on seeing itself disfigured, comes to know itself in its truth, which it otherwise seeks to hide by every means possible. The reality of the crucified peoples appears also by means of copro-analysis: the feces show what the First World produces, its state of health and its truth.[67]

Even if that light of truth is unappealing, disdaining and discarding it is senseless. Science analyzes reality, but in order to see reality as it is, it first needs light. The light that comes from the poor is what makes it possible to overcome voluntary blindness.[68] This light can awaken people from the dogmatic dream to which the West has succumbed: the dream about its own reality. That was how Ellacuría saw it, and in Central American University he recommended that people at least try to "work from the light and in the light that the world's oppressed majorities throw on the whole world, for the blinding of some, but for the illumination of others."[69]

What I am allowed to hope for. Poor people give new life to utopian vision, which was so valued by Ernst Bloch and is now so devalued by postmodernity. Moreover, the poor project such a vision in a precise way. "Utopia" means a dignified and just life for the majorities; it is not the (impossible) ideal of social and political perfection, conceived out of abundance, as in the republics of Plato or Thomas More or Campanella (utopias that are naturalist, theocratic, and aristocratically communist).

The poor transform the very notion of a historical utopia, which is their most important contribution: for them it is not a question of *ou-topia,* that "no-place" that does not exist, but of *eu-topia,* that "good place" that must exist. What we call the "good life," "quality of life," "welfare state"—prosperity for the minorities—are feats along the road toward the utopia that is conceived out of the abundance of the nonpoor. But of course they are feats with which they are not content, so that they unleash a frantic race for progress. This is the flight forward, despite the presence of a humanity in crisis. In contrast, the utopia of the poor is the *oikos,* the existence and the guarantee of an essential core of basic life and of human family.

Correlatively, from the poor comes hope, *true* hope—that is, the way to hope. In the "world of abundance" there exist expectations, which are extrapolated on the basis of calculations, but there is not a radical break between the present and the future. That's fine, but it is not hope, for, in the Christian sense at least, true hope is hoping against hope. The root of hope is not in objective calculation; neither is it in subjective optimism. Rather it is in love, which bears all. The hope of the poor passes through crises, through epochs of "disenchantment with the immediate," for there do not appear any "immediate and calculable outcomes and victories."[70] But there is a faith that overcomes darkness, and there is a hope that triumphs over disenchantment, as is well shown in poor people's historic patience and their determination to live. It is what we call primordial holiness. That hope is precisely what they offer to the First World. Ellacuría used to say of the First World, comparing it with the hope he saw in Latin America: "The only thing they really have is fear."[71]

What I have to do. The poor mark out the direction and the basic contents of our practice. Let us consider this in what are today two necessary points. The first is that, correlatively to the truth that the poor express and require, they make possible true prophetic condemnation. The profound truth they reveal is that, more than anything else, condemnation is necessary in order to be in tune with reality, that is, in order to be real. For that reason, minimizing the need for prophecy and discrediting it as mere "protest" is a serious error. We must go beyond psychology. By its nature, prophetic condemnation means becoming an echo of a reality that wishes to speak forth. Condemnation means "being the voice of a reality that is oppressed and, moreover, deprived of a voice." If mere protest is something easy, as is sometimes simplistically or cynically supposed, such is not the case with prophetic condemnation. It is costly, for to echo reality you have to be in it (incarnation), you have to see it as it is (honesty with what is real), and above all you have to be moved to mercy and decide to work for justice (taking responsibility for the real), by accepting the inevitable consequences of persecution and even of death (bearing the real).[72]

The second point is that the intolerability of poverty requires a dynamic not only for condemning it, but for creating economic, political, and cultural models that overcome it, as Ellacuría used to say. In this sense, "there is no protest without a corresponding proposal." In any case, the poor demand that the new models not be inhumane or dehumanizing.

Signs and Leaven

The poor, as persons and as communities, have remarkable values that are generally ignored: resistance, simplicity, joy in life's basic elements, openness to the mystery of God, and so on; recall the earlier citations of Comblin, Ronaldo Muñoz, and Felix Wilfred. With those values they give new shapes to society, as modest as they may seem to outsiders. In my view, these values are above all in the line of humanization. They are important for living more humanly, but they also facilitate the production of basic goods.

The poor offer models, sometimes small ones, sometimes notable ones—but *their own* models—of grassroots economics, community organization, health care, housing, human rights, education, culture, religion, politics, arts, sports. . . . In many cultures they possess a great ecological consciousness, and they take care of nature and Mother Earth in ways far superior to the ways of the West.

Furthermore the poor, depending on places and circumstances, organize themselves into people's liberation movements, even revolutionary ones. They accumulate social and/or political power, depending on the issues. They do so to defend their own rights, but also to defend the rights of other poor and oppressed people, and sometimes the rights of a whole people. They seek and sometimes obtain power. Such a victory then makes them run the risk of dehumanization, but often they show a great, humanizing generosity. And they get results.

To put it plainly, the poor have values and produce positive realities and new social forms that, even if not given massive expression, do offer orientations and elements for a new society. At times they do not stay enclosed in their own communities, but appear as a sign for others. Like the lamp in the gospel, they illuminate their surroundings. They can then become the salt that gives flavor and the leaven that makes the dough expand, which means that they produce salvation beyond themselves. This quality is what Ellacuría used to find in poor people's communities, especially in the base communities:

> There are signs that the poor are evangelizers, that they are saviors. The splendid experience of the base communities, as a ferment of Church renovation and as a factor of political transformation, and the frequent example of "poor people with spirit"—who organize in order to struggle in solidarity and in martyrdom for the good of their brothers and sisters, for the most humble and the weakest—already give proof of the salvific and liberating potential of the poor.[73]

The Convocation to the Solidarity of the Human Family

The poor unleash solidarity, which, as has been said so beautifully, is "the tenderness of the peoples." We have defined it as "unequals bearing one another mutually." But we need to analyze the concept in depth and see what poor people contribute to it. Solidarity means poor people and nonpoor people mutually bearing one another, giving "to each other" and receiving "from each other" the best that they have, in order to arrive at being "with one another."[74] Often what is given and what is received are in quite different orders of reality: material aid and human acceptance, for example. And what the nonpoor receive may be, as a humanizing reality, superior to what they give. This kind of solidarity goes beyond mere unilateral aid, with its intrinsic tendency toward imposition and domination. It also goes beyond alliances between those who wish to defend their own common interests over against other people's interests.

Understanding solidarity in the sense of unequals bearing one another mutually is something novel, but such solidarity is necessary in a world of unequals; it can resolve the ambiguity and root out what is harmful in the falsely universalizing concept of globalization. Most importantly, the source of solidarity thus understood and the call to practice it do not come from just anywhere; they come from the poor. Historically such solidarity happens locally, in small ways, through what has happened in places like El Salvador or Nicaragua, but it makes an immense contribution to our understanding of true solidarity, especially now with the proliferation of aid organizations and ideologies, private and governmental, religious and secular. It seems to me most important that such organizations operate according to the objective dynamic of bearing one another mutually, and not according to the self-interested directives of the United Nations, the European Community, and others.

Victims and Redemption

Historically, the poor are victims, and as such they also shape the process of liberation, now in the form of redemption. Archbishop Romero, without pretending to theological precision, said with brilliant insight, "Among the poor Christ desired to place his seat of redemption" (Homily of December 24, 1978).

The term "redemption" is ignored today, as if it explained nothing important about how to heal a sick world; but it explains a lot. In the process of salvation it is necessary to eliminate many evils, and it is necessary to struggle against the structures that produce them. When the evil is profound, enduring, and structural, however, it is necessary to eradicate evils in order truly to heal. This task is so difficult that it has always been thought to require an extraordinary effort, something outside the normal. In metaphoric language this has been expressed by saying that, in order to heal a corrupt world, it is necessary to "pay a price," which is precisely the etymological meaning of "redemption," *redemptio*. In other words, besides the normal labors and sufferings involved in the production of goods, "adding on" something burdensome is a necessity. In more historical language, we might say that to eradicate the roots of evil, we must struggle against evil not only from without, but from within, ready to allow evil to grind us up. Here there appears the "extra" suffering that in history is always related to redemption.

In El Salvador we have often said as much, in the presence of violence. This violence must be combated in diverse ways: from without, as it were, with ideas, negotiations, and even, tragically and in extreme cases, with other violence, making use of it in the most humane way possible. But in order to redeem violence we must combat it also from within, that is, be ready to bear with it. All the martyrs for justice have borne witness to this: Gandhi, Martin Luther King, Archbishop Romero. . . . Ignacio Ellacuría had just such a premonition on September 19, 1989, two months before becoming a victim of violence himself. In the presence of presidents Óscar Arias of Costa Rica and Alfredo Cristiani of El Salvador, he gave a frankly political speech aimed at moving negotiations forward; he stated, apparently without intending religious overtones:

> There has been much pain suffered and much blood shed, but now the classical *theologoumenon "nulla redemptio sine efussione sanguinis"* reminds us again that the salvation and the liberation of the peoples takes place through very painful sacrifices.[75]

This redemption thesis should be understood well. We are not defending any Anselmian theory, as if suffering were necessary—and effective—for placating the divine wrath and obtaining salvation.[76] In order to save, God does not require a sacrifice that kills his creatures, and therefore there is no need to seek out excellent victims for sacrifice. This would mean that the victims' suffering, by its nature, would "disarm" the power of evil, not magically, but historically. This is a way of trying to explain conceptually the saving element of Christ's suffering on the cross: sin has discharged all its force against him, but in doing so sin itself has been left without force. So it is not that suffering placates God and makes him benevolent; rather what it does is disarm evil. As for God, the cross is proof of his love, since he accepted us precisely at the moment when he could have rejected us, because of the suffering we have inflicted on his Son.

Nor do we seek to defend any kind of sacrificialism, as if suffering in itself were something good for human beings. We do insist on venerating the victims who suffer, because in them there is much of the mystery that is *fascinans et tremens*. And we insist on gratitude, for often such suffering accompanies or follows on great generosity and supreme love. We venerate and give thanks for a positive, primordial reality: in this cruel world, and opposed to it, true love has appeared.

Redemption continues to be a *mysterium magnum*, but sometimes a miracle happens, and the mystery appears visibly as a *mysterium salutis*. Of this we can speak only with fear and trembling, and above all we should speak through our decision to give life to the victims and to pledge our own life in that endeavor. Still, we should not ignore the salvific potential of such a mystery, out of respect for the victims, but also out of a properly understood self-interest, namely, not to impoverish ourselves even more. As we have already seen, the innocent victims save precisely by moving us to conversion, to being honest with reality, to having hope, to practicing solidarity. . . . And sometimes, even amid horrors, immediate and tangible fruits of salvation are miraculously produced, like leaven that humanizes the dough. It is the miracle of a redemption that is offered and received.

> In Auschwitz, prisoner denies prisoner, but Father [Maximilian] Kolbe breaks with that norm: *prisoner offers his life for another prisoner who is unknown to him.* . . . Although the Enlightenment—so rational and rationalizing—could never comprehend such an act, even in Auschwitz it is possible to live from loving grace in dialogue with the light . . . , to encourage the hope and remove the despair of the others sentenced to the cell of punishment.[77]

"After Auschwitz we are able to continue praying because in Auschwitz they also prayed,"[78] according to the memorable words of J. B. Metz, one who was not at all given to naïve theodicy. And Etty Hillesum put down in writing what she was hoping for in Auschwitz: "to help God as much as possible."[79] Suffering has wrought redemption.

The Great Lakes region of Africa is the Auschwitz of today, and there also an incredible humanity has been engendered. "It is not difficult to sing and give praise when everything is assured. The marvel is that . . . the prisoners of Kigali, who today will receive visits by relatives, who with great travail bring them something to eat, can still bless and give thanks to God. How can they not be the favored ones, those from whom we must learn the meaning of gratuity! Today I received a letter from them. Perhaps they do not realize how much we receive from them and how they save us."[80]

When the Peace Accords were signed in El Salvador in 1992, it was insisted that the peace was an achievement of the martyrs and the fallen. But beyond the great truth of these words, though it is often distorted, there is also the truth that, as in Auschwitz and in the Great Lakes, the "extra" of the victims' suffering has generated redemption, an offer of humanization. In a Salvadoran refugee camp during the war, on the Day of the Dead, some *campesinos* prayed for their murdered relatives and also for the murderers. They said: "You know, we believed that they also, the enemy, should have been on the altar. They are our brothers despite the fact that they kill us and murder us. Of course you know the

Bible says: it is easy to love your own, but God asks that we also love those who persecute us."[81] We do not know whether the murderers ever came to receive that offer of salvation that the victims made to them, or whether they accepted it. But with that prayer for the assassins and with other proofs of the victims' love, the world became impregnated with humanity—a capital that should not be squandered, but rather should be put to work, like a great treasure.

That treasure is grace. And if we ask why it should be mentioned in talking about the salvation of a sick society, then we have not understood Jesus of Nazareth, nor human beings, nor the society we live in, which is bursting with sin, but is also teeming with the grace of the victims. We come to be truly human not only by making our own selves—often in Promethean fashion—but by letting ourselves be made human by others. That is the gift dimension of salvation.

But our times don't seem right for talking this way. Society's ideal—comprehensible, but dangerous—is to save only by producing goods, as if all evils will gradually disappear by themselves, without leaving scars and without activating sin's particular dynamic of "returning," of *coming back* to produce more death and inhumanity. For that reason, it is not possible to speak of salvation without keeping present the historical need for redemption.

This point appears quite clearly when we analyze what the martyrs of our time bring about.[82] Today the great entrepreneurs of redemption are the Jesuanic martyrs, taken as a whole; they include both the active martyrs, who live and die like Jesus, and those who are made to die slowly through unjust poverty and/or violence, in massacres, anonymously, in groups and in collective bodies. Strictly speaking, the second are more redeeming than the first, though often no clear dividing line between them is apparent. They all bear the sin of the world, and they weaken the roots of evil, though they never finally eradicate them. Thus do they bring about salvation.

In order to see things this way faith is needed, just as it was in the case of the suffering servant of Yahweh. Sometimes, though, the testimony occurs in verifiable fashion. The case of Archbishop Romero is paradigmatic. A bishop, pursued by the local powers of every sort, murdered innocently and defenselessly by mercenaries in connivance with the empire, generated new hope, fostered new commitment, and called forth an unprecedented universal solidarity.[83] And Archbishop Romero was not just a single individual. Rather, it may well be said that he was the most visible head of a whole people that was struggling against the sin of the world and bearing that sin.

Without making light of the problem of theodicy, on the one hand, or falling into victimology, on the other, we believe that in the immense pain of the victims there is "something" that can heal our world. We approve of Ivan Karamazov's gesture of refusing to enter a heaven to which people must ascend to recover lost harmony. But we do accept entrance into a destroyed earth, to which we must descend in order to find "something" of humanity. Seeking suffering in order to find salvation would be blasphemy.[84] But in the presence of the victims' suffering, it is arrogance to refuse to open up to their salvific power and let ourselves be embraced by them.

Redemption is necessary. "Linking the future of humanity with the fate of the poor has become a historical necessity. . . . Only the victims can redeem the future."[85] And it is possible. As on the cross of Christ, likewise in history, suffering and total love can be united. Then love saves. As Nelly Sachs says, "They loved so much they made the granite of the night jump and break into pieces."[86]

The Analogy of Being "In the World of the Poor"

So how much salvation can arise in the world of the nonpoor? Undoubtedly, the nonpoor can cooperate in healing a gravely ill society, but on one condition: that they participate really and historically, not just intentionally and spiritually, in the world of the poor.

Many goods are produced among the nonpoor: the science of Pasteur and Einstein; the revolution of "liberty, equality, and fraternity"; the universal declarations of human rights; economic models that can indeed overcome poverty; plus the political power that can make them work. And that can be said as well for the globalization we have already criticized.[87] We are not going to belabor the point.

The nonpoor may also be necessary to make effective the salvation that comes from the poor. They can become prophetic figures who help the poor to recover and maintain confidence in themselves, to develop practices and to spread hope. When such figures do not appear, frustration may increase among the poor, but when they do appear, the community of the poor is empowered and creates an even greater ferment. These prophetic figures may come from among the poor, but also from among the nonpoor. *Archbishop* Romero and *university president* Ellacuría were not from the world of the poor. But as they lowered themselves, they received salvation, and the poor became empowered as saviors.

Left to itself, however, there is no evidence that the world of abundance can bring salvation, and normally the salvation it brings is totally ambiguous: Hiroshima or useful energy? Nourishment and health or individualistic consumerism and spiritless commodification? Universalization or conquest? Such salvation usually arrives mixed with sinfulness: imposition, violence, and the arrogant pretension of beneficence. For salvation to come from this world, it is not enough just to produce goods and heap them on top of the evils; rather it is necessary to purify their ambiguity and cleanse their sinfulness. The world of the nonpoor is capable of attempting both these tasks: it presents proposals that are generally ethical, humanistic, and religious. But the most radical possibility, without which the others are usually not sufficient, consists in lowering ourselves to what is poor in history.

This does not usually happen by our own initiative; it happens only by the encouraging invitation, or by the actual pressure, that comes from the world of the poor. It is difficult, but it can occur, and in diverse ways. The heart of the matter is our participating in some way, analogously, but truly, in the reality of the world of the poor.

This can happen in many forms: by actual, comradely *insertion* in that world, by unequivocal *service* on its behalf, by liberating *praxis* alongside the poor, by running *risks* to defend them, by assuming their *fate* of persecution and death, by sharing *their joys and their hopes*. All this is real and verifiable, not just intentional. And when such participation really takes place, as analogous as it may be, then salvation can come also from the world of abundance. But we must be clear about what analogy does not include: it does not consist in mere intentionality that is unsullied by real poverty. Some people believe that there is no longer any need to participate in that world nowadays; they hold that a well-managed self-interest is sufficient to bring salvation, so that no significant cost is necessarily involved. It's the bargain of our times: in order to save, there is no need for generosity or sacrifice. It recalls the old fallacy: that it is enough to be "poor in spirit," without any sort of participation in real poverty.[88]

Extra Pauperes Nulla Salus

We could have written all the foregoing without mentioning at all the formula *extra pauperes nulla salus*. Moreover, this formula appears nowhere in either traditional or progressive theology. It does not even appear in liberation theology, as far as the phrasing goes, although it is quite coherent with it. We use this formula because, as such, it has historical antecedents that go back to the *extra ecclesiam nulla salus* of Origen and Cyprian, and because it defines in radical fashion the problem of the locus of salvation.

After Vatican II, Schillebeeckx wrote: *extra mundum nulla salus, outside the world there is no salvation*, as a way of rephrasing the traditional formulation. By that he meant that "the world and the human history in which God works salvation are the bases of the whole reality of faith; it is in the world, first of all, that salvation is attained or damnation is consummated. In this sense, it is true that *extra mundum nulla salus*."[89] Thus, in his analysis of the place of salvation, Schillebeeckx made the globalizing *caesura* effected by the council into something productive.[90] The new formula overcomes the danger of exclusivism that is found in the rigorist interpretation: not only the Church, but also the world is the place of salvation.[91] It also overcomes the danger of reductionism: salvation is not only religious, but also has a historical and social dimension.[92]

This conciliar *caesura* was an epochal novelty, comparable only with the much earlier council—or rather, assembly—of Jerusalem, where it was decided that salvation was possible for all human beings, without having to pass through Judaism. This put an end to Jewish religious exclusivism. With good reason did Rahner claim that Vatican II had been the most important council in all the Church's history since the Council of Jerusalem.

Shortly afterward, however, around the time of Medellín, there occurred an even greater *caesura*, one that also affected our understanding of salvation and the place where it happens. Medellin was a fruit of Vatican II, one of the more important ones, if not the most important,[93] but it also surpassed the council. The fundamental advance was that it now related faith and the Church not to the world, but to the poor. And it did the same with theology. In terms of the intellectual task, Medellín granted the poor a status of hermeneutical privilege; that is, Medellín prioritized the ability to understand realities and texts from their perspective, precisely what liberation theology did. Medellín insisted that all the contents of theology should be seen in relation to the poor. Thus did it proclaim "the Church of the poor," a conception that in the council had barely been touched, despite the attempts of John XXIII, Cardinal Lercaro, and Bishop Himmer of Tournay with their formula, *primus locus in Ecclesia pauperibus reservandus est*. And in a peak moment for *theo*-logy, Archbishop Romero reformulated the famous sentence of Irenaeus: *gloria Dei vivens pauper*.[94] From among the poor he reformulated the mystery of God—and I believe that even now we have been incapable of assimilating his novelty and boldness; we still reduce his words to eloquent rhetorical flourishes. For its part, theology also asked in radical fashion about the locus for finding God. Porfirio Miranda responded, "The question is not whether or not someone looks for God, but whether he looks for God where God himself said he was."[95] In the poor of this world.

From the theological dynamic of "from among the poor," there developed also a rethinking of the locus from which salvation comes. In this way we arrived at the formula *extra pauperes nulla salus* (outside the poor there is no salvation). I read the formula for the first time in Javier Vitoria's doctoral thesis on Christian salvation from the perspective of liberation theology[96] and then later in González-Faus's analysis of what remained of liberation theology,[97] as some people were wondering a few years ago. As far as I recall, Ellacuría did not use that formula precisely, but in proposing the civilization of poverty as an expression of the kingdom of God, he had the same intuition: he related poor people to the "place" of salvation (a categorical *ubi*: "outside of them") and to the "contents" of salvation (a substantial *quid*: "what salvation"). Furthermore he recovered a central truth by making it historical: salvation comes from the suffering servant of Yahweh. Finally, he recovered redemption as an essential dimension of salvation: it is necessary to produce goods, but it is also necessary to eradicate evils, by taking them on.[98]

Let us return to the formula. We already said that it is countercultural, since the world of wealth believes that it already possesses "salvation" and the means that lead to it, precisely in virtue of its not being the world of the poor. It cannot conceive that salvation might come to it from without, much less from the poor. Whether saved or damned, says the world of wealth, "Reality is us." This is the hubris that Paul denounces.

The formula is also defenseless before the objections presented by history and reason, but it is necessary, at least as therapy for a society that is suffering a "moral and humanitarian failure."[99] The formula should not be discredited simply because the *mysterium iniquitatis* is present also among the poor. Even the church fathers of antiquity called the Church *casta meretrix*, the chaste prostitute. The Church is not the place of salvation because it has no sin in it,[100] but because of the presence of Christ and his spirit in it, which will always produce life and holiness, an effective way of expressing faith. Something similar may be said of the world of the poor—though here also faith becomes analogous. Besides their raw reality, in the poor there will always be something of the spirit. Further, what is not just possibility, but essential affirmation, is that in the poor there will always be something of Christ. Both Medellín and Puebla insisted on that in radical fashion, referring to Matthew 25: Christ "has desired to identify himself with the poorest and the weakest in the most tender way" (Puebla, no. 196).[101]

The Mystery of the Poor

Even as we conclude these reflections, we still feel the disquiet, mentioned at the start, that is produced by the novelty and the scandalous aspect of the topic. We are aware of many limitations. We have not offered a sufficiently satisfactory concept of salvation,[102] nor have we defined well enough the different ways that the poor and the nonpoor bring about salvation. On the one hand, the nonpoor save more by way of producing goods and knowledge for individual and community enjoyment; on the other, the poor save more by way of "inspiration," "attraction," and "impulse," by causing "ferment" and by providing modest models for a different type of society. I also believe that it is necessary to analyze more in depth the relation between the simply "needy poor" and the "poor with spirit."

Having said this, though, I feel sure about one thing. There will be no salvation or humanization if redemptive impulses do not emerge from that world of the poor. What the domineering and arrogant "world of the nonpoor" produces can generate no salvation, if it does not in some way pass through the "world of the poor." To put it in the form of a maxim: salvation and humanization will come about only "with" the poor. "Without" the poor there will come no salvation that is humane.

The disquiet we allude to remains with us, and we recall the words of Ellacuría about the suffering servant, chosen by God to bring salvation: "Only by a difficult act of faith is the one who sings about the servant able to discover what appears to be totally contrary to the eyes of history."[103] Similarly, only by a difficult act of faith—even if it is a reflective faith—are we able to accept that in the poor there is salvation and outside of them there is not. The reason is that the world of the poor places us before a mystery, and they themselves express a mystery.

The *Mysterium Iniquitatis: Evil and Wickedness*

First of all, to ward off accusations of naïveté, we recognize the *mysterium iniquitatis* that is present in the world of the poor. We see there deficiencies that reinforce the selfishness that is part of every human being, the contamination of the imagination by offerings that come from the North—even though the poor have every right to enjoy the benefits of civilization that are within their reach—and simple wickedness: abuse, rape, gross machismo, deceit, mutilation, massacre, and sometimes larger human catastrophes.

In recent epochs, the members of the security forces and the members of the resistance organizations were all poor people, and Archbishop Romero bitterly bemoaned the fact that the very same factor uniting them, the need to survive, also separated them, to the point where they killed one another. Right now something similar is happening with the youth gangs to an appallingly aberrant degree: they are all basically poor people slaughtering one another. Fourteen years after the Peace Accords, in a country of 6 million inhabitants, we have an average of twelve homicides a day.

Mysterium iniquitatis is the tragedy of Rwanda and the Great Lakes region, for which the North has a long-standing responsibility, compounded by its present-day insensibility, but for which the African peoples are also responsible. Congolese Bishop Melchisedec Sikuli recognizes this in enumerating the huge problems that distress his country: poverty, injustice, displacement of persons, rape of women, sacking of villages, all against the background of the sin of colonialism. But he does not hide the evils of Africans, which he illustrates with the drama of the child-soldiers, even though his compassion in the face of so much suffering moves him to seek some type of explanation. He cites, vulnerably, some words from the book of Kouroma, *Allah is not Happy*: "When you don't have anyone at all in the world, neither father nor mother nor sister, and you are still a child, living in a barbarous, destroyed country where everybody kills everybody, what do you do? You become a child soldier in order to eat and to kill: that is the only option left to us."[104]

There is no need, then, for idealizing anyone, but neither is there any room for hypocrisy, as when the world of abundance recalls—even if with a badly disguised air of superiority—the horrors of the world of the poor, ultimately in order to avoid taking seriously its own atrocities: Auschwitz, Hiroshima, the Gulag, Vietnam, Iraq, the national security regimes . . . What certainly remains is the question: Why, Lord, why?

The Mysterium Salutis: *Primordial Holiness*

Despite all this, the poor who have suffered so much oppression and repression, in our country, in Central Asia, in the Great Lakes region; the mothers who after a catastrophe hold fast to their children's hands and carry all their possessions on top of their heads, seeking refuge, journeying hundreds of kilometers in mile-long caravans; the people sick with AIDS, who only want to die with dignity; and so many others who have struggled against oppression in all its varied forms—despite all this, I say, these people are still capable of resistance and celebration.

About the prisons and the refugee camps there are many tales of cruelty and misery, but what is incredible is that there are also tales of love, of hope, of longing to live and help others, of grassroots organizing, both religious and secular, for the sake of pronouncing their word and maintaining their dignity. Teresa Florensa, a religious who has worked in the Great Lakes region, writes:

> These human beings continue to be the refuse of humanity. There are millions of people, too many in our world. Nobody knows what to do with them, and they know that they don't count for anybody. Stuck to their skin they have a whole history of suffering, humiliation, terror, hunger and death. They are sorely wounded in their dignity. . . . But this work with the refugees of the Great Lakes is also an invitation to trust in human beings and their ability to overcome even the worst conditions.

For the nonpoor people of the world of abundance, this can produce shock and guilt ("What have you made of your brother?"), but, even more, it should produce respect and veneration. We have given a name to this striving for survival—and for peaceable sharing with others—in the midst of great sufferings, and to the labors to achieve this with creativity, dignity, resistance, and limitless fortitude, defying tremendous obstacles: we have called all this primordial holiness.[105] Unlike the official kind of sanctity, this type is not judged in terms of what it possesses by virtue of freedom or necessity, of virtue or obligation, of grace or merit. It has no need to be accompanied by heroic virtues, but it expresses itself in a life that is completely heroic. Such primordial holiness invites us to a mutual giving, a mutual receiving, and a mutual celebration of the joy of being human.

I have asked myself if the wickedness and the holiness described above are the same as those found in the world of wealth, and I believe there are real differences, at least as far as they affect me personally. The wickedness of the world of the poor appears "less" wicked, for it is the result of the need to survive and the desperation of a life of chronic misery. There is always freedom, or crumbs of freedom, one might say, but such freedom exists in the midst of vulnerability, weakness, and the oppression that comes from society and its institutions. The poor are those who have (almost) all the powers of this world arrayed against them. For that reason I do not find it easy to accept a total historical symmetry between the poor and the nonpoor, between their concupiscence and the original sin they remind us of.

In like manner, holiness from below appears to be "more" holiness. To paraphrase freely from Kant's *Metaphysics of Morals*, where he distinguishes between "worth" and "dignity," I believe that in the world of wealth, even one possessing dignity, the culture of "worth" tends to prevail, whereas in the world of poverty "dignity" predominates. Jesus said that the poor widow had given more than all the rest, for she had given out of her poverty. She had given "all." The difference is not in the quantity, but in the quality. The poor do not have money, and so with much greater ease they can give themselves.

We have stated that there exists a disproportion in the gross inequality between the rich man and the poor Lazarus, but there also exists a disproportionate difference of dignity between the two. Poor people are, often enough, the true "shepherds of being." Certainly, they are "guardians of dignity" and "aristocrats of the spirit," as Jon Cortina used to say.

This world of the poor is what produced Ellacuría's hopeful exultation, both utopian and realistic. He knew well the difficulties, but he discerned also "the immense spiritual and human richness of the poor and the Third World peoples, a richness now stifled by misery and by the imposition of cultural models that are in some ways more developed, but not for that reason more fully human."[106] That richness is drowned in a thousand problems, but it is not eliminated. And very often it shines forth radiantly.

The Mystery of God in the Poor

And in the poor one glimpses God. Let us say this in conclusion, using some cherished words of Gustavo Gutiérrez.

In the midst of the suffering of the innocent, it is asked "how to speak of God from Ayacucho,"[107] a Peruvian city whose name in Quechua means "corner of the dead." Here, those asking for God are Job, Ivan Karamazov, Jesus on the cross.

And from among the poor comes the answer, in the well-known verses of the Peruvian poet César Vallejo: "The lottery seller who shouts 'One for a thousand!' contains an unfathomable depth of God."[108] Here the answer comes from the Roman centurion at the foot of the cross: "Truly this man was the Son of God!" (Mark 15:39). He has found God.

The poor have recourse to God because God is in them, hidden and at the same time manifest. And they are "vicars of Christ."

On the eve of the Fifth Latin American Bishops Conference, in Aparecida, Brazil, I end this essay by offering a text of Ignacio Ellacuría that throws light on what should be the nature and the function of the Latin American Churches. It is a text on the option for the poor, and it is also a text on the option of letting ourselves be saved by them.

> The great salvific task, then, is to evangelize the poor so that out of their material poverty they may attain the awareness and the spirit necessary, first to escape from their indigence and oppression, second to put an end to the oppressive structures, and third to inaugurate a new heaven and a new earth, where sharing trumps accumulating and where there is time to hear and enjoy God's voice in the heart of the material world and in the heart of human history. The poor will save the world; they are already saving it, though not yet. Seeking salvation by some other road is a dogmatic and historical error. If this means to hope against all hope, it is most definitely a sure guarantee that all this will be attained some day. The poor continue to be the world's great reservoir of human hope and spirituality.[109]

—Translated by Joseph Owens

4

The Centrality of the Kingdom of God Announced by Jesus

Reflections before Aparecida

The kingdom of God announced by Jesus is central to Christian life and the Church's mission. It is not present, however, in the *Participation Document* sent out by way of preparation for the Fifth Latin American Bishops' Conference, which will take place in Aparecida, Brazil, in May 2007. In the document's Christology, the concrete Jesus of Nazareth practically disappears, in favor of an abstract Christ. The result, in the words of Agenor Brighenti, is an "eclipse of the kingdom of God" in our understanding of what the Church is and does.

We will not analyze here in detail all that the kingdom of God meant for Jesus; nor will we treat the "kingdom of Christ," which is also important in the New Testament. Among several possible topics, we will develop three themes with deep roots in the Gospels; all three are closely related to the kingdom and may throw light on our reflections about Aparecida. These themes are utopia, the poor, and the following of Jesus. If we as Christians and if the Churches incorporate these into our life and mission, then Christianity will be, even today, good news for the world. Otherwise, we believe, it will not be easy.

The Centrality of the Kingdom of God

We begin with a brief reflection on the centrality of the kingdom of God in the Scriptures, its formal and material content, and its basic characteristics.

Originally published in *Revista Latinoamericana de Teología* 68 (2006): 135–60.

The kingdom of God is central in the Old Testament tradition as a way of expressing God's salvific plan and the people's hope. Indeed, Israel passed through innumerable vicissitudes, problems, and tragedies, but it always maintained a hope based on its faith. Israel did not relegate God to a nebulous beyond, but experienced God passing through its history, and in very concrete ways. In Egypt God heard the cries of an oppressed people and came down to liberate them. That liberation was the origin of their hope and their confession of faith. They formulated their hope and faith in terms of royalty and kingdom. "Now he comes to rule the earth; he will rule the world with justice and the peoples with truth" (Ps. 96:13).

When God reigns, the world becomes the kingdom of God; therefore, rather than speak of a kingdom, we should speak of the reign of God. As to its content, that reign brings about, above all, the longed-for ideal of justice. "God shows that he reigns in the world by the fact that, since he is good and merciful with all his creatures (cf. Ps 86:15f.; Ps 145:9), he transforms an unjust socio-historic reality into one that is just, one in which solidarity reigns and there are no poor people (cf. Deut 15:4)."[1] Accordingly, the reign of God should be understood not just as beneficent action, but as liberating and as partisan, since oppressed people are—by right—at the center of God's regard and God's action. Further, God's reign has a historical dimension, since it concerns liberation from objective forms of oppression, though its vision keeps opening up onto transcendence; it has a social dimension, since it is liberation and justice for a people, even when its vision also touches individual persons. As we have said also, God's reign is theologal, since God reveals his reality in passing in this way, and not another, through history.

But this kingdom, which is a gift of God, becomes also a task for the people; this aspect is central in the Scriptures, and it is most important that we recall this today as we reflect on the Church's mission. In other words, God's way of acting—having compassion, doing justice, liberating—should also be Israel's way of acting: "There shall not be any poor among you, you shall share the fruits of the harvest with the poorest, you will help the stranger and the widow" (cf. Deut. 15; 16; Lev. 19). Only by acting this way, not just by being chosen, will Israel truly be God's people. Being chosen does not mean a privileged status that places Israel over and above other peoples. Rather, being chosen entails a serious responsibility, and understanding it in this way is important, since the very awareness of "being chosen" always brings with it grave dangers—for the Church as well. We do well to recall, therefore, that the Old Testament does not shy away from affirming that God also liberated the Philistines from Kaftor and the Arameans from Kir (Amos 9:7ff.).

And God will liberate—indeed!—the Egyptians, the same ones from whom he liberated Israel: "When they cry to Yahweh because of oppressors, he will send them a savior and will defend and deliver them. And Yahweh will make himself known to the Egyptians; and the Egyptians will know Yahweh in that day" (Isa. 19:20–21). The conclusion is that God can work wonders with any people—something worth keeping in mind in our interreligious dialogue. Election, therefore, is not purely arbitrary, nor is it an excuse for not doing that which is required of all human beings. To the contrary, there is a need to respond to election, by acting in history just as God has acted with the chosen. It is not, then, just some "cheap grace."

Let us say, finally, that the reign of God also has a personal dimension. God reigns when human beings, "made in the image and likeness of God," reproduce in their lives the goodness and the compassion, the justice and the reconciliation of God. God reigns when the heart of stone is transformed into a heart of flesh (Ezekiel), when human beings come to know Yahweh intimately (Jeremiah). . . .

Out of that same tradition came Jesus. He announced the imminent arrival of that kingdom, and he gave signs of its presence: healings, expulsion of demons, welcome of sinners and outcasts, meals with them. . . . He was the good news of God, *eu-angelion*—especially for the poor. He placed himself at their service and defended them from their oppressors until his death on the cross. And even in the midst of deep darkness, he maintained his hope in the coming of the kingdom. At the end he thought that it would arrive a little after his death, and that his death might even hasten its coming. After his death his disciples recognized that, in Jesus, God was now reigning in history: Jesus "went about doing good and healing all who were oppressed by the devil," which they interpreted as God's passing through: "for God was with him" (Acts 10:38).

The Gospels show more clearly than the Old Testament how God's reign extends not just over a people, but over individual persons. Jesus announces the good news to very concrete persons and makes it real for them. He also requires of them, personally, a way of life that will make God reign in Israel. He requires that they follow him, that they act out the reign, and that they mold themselves according to the message and the person of Jesus himself, along the line of the parables of the Good Samaritan, the Prodigal Son, the Beatitudes. . . . And he also requires them to share in his destiny: being persecuted and crucified for prophetically confronting the world of oppression.

Finally, Jesus invites his followers to call God *abba*, as he himself did, and to relate to God as a personal reality of refreshing, scandalous goodness, who embraces them with tenderness and unconditional acceptance. He also requires his followers to let *abba* be "God," mystery beyond manipulation, who may demand of them prophetic condemnation, involvement in conflicts, courting of dangers, and also uncertainty, journeys along unknown paths, availability up to the end, up to the "My God, why have you abandoned me?" This was the way that Jesus' followers were to be, so that Paul could so splendidly proclaim that God's design is that "we come to be children in the Son." In this way does God reign over persons.

Let us now examine some important realities which, so to speak, orbit around God's kingdom, and whose existence is in danger of being ignored or diminished when we forget about the kingdom.

UTOPIA

Hope and Utopia

In announcing that the kingdom was drawing near, Jesus brought hope, above all to the poor. We therefore begin by asking how hope—even more, utopian hope—fares today, in the world and in theology.

Not so long ago it was still stylish to speak of hope, and even of utopias. From Europe came the longing of Bloch: "that the world might become a home for man." In Latin America some used to speak of "revolution," and Medellín spoke of "liberation from all forms of slavery." Utopia and hope were alive, but capitalism adulterated them: Fukuyama was claiming that the end of history had already arrived, and nowadays, though such language is no longer used, attempts are made to convince us that the utopia is arriving with globalization.

Whether by way of criticism or cynicism, postmodern thought has discredited the utopian vision; it has put an end to the great narratives and advises us to be more reasonable and to make do with less grandiose narratives. For rich people all this signifies moderation (a quite worthy suggestion if only it were made with commitment to a universal social perspective that would lead to a civilization of austerity), while for poor people it means resignation (wherein is expressed the cruelty of our civilization: condemning the majorities to live without hope, almost the way Dante describes the sign at the gates of hell: "Leave behind all hope, ye who enter this place"). But postmodernism should be quite aware that the "great narratives" are still prominent in our world—negatively, to be sure—in Africa, Central Asia, and Latin America in general.[2] For other reasons (disenchantment, reverses, involution, imposition, and centralism in the ecclesial sphere), the hope inspired by Medellín also gradually lost its force, although there still remain a good number of communities, now more muted, along with the resistance movements of "another world is possible," which keep growing. Bishop Pedro Casaldáliga keeps making his profession of faith: "Utopia [is] as necessary as the daily bread." He also formulates it in more daring fashion: "We Christians are an army of defeated soldiers fighting for an invincible cause."

Let us consider now the good news. In the Gospels, the kingdom is utopia, but a specific utopia that needs to be described well. It relates not to just any lack or limitation in human beings, but specifically to the suffering of the poor. What corresponds to such a utopia is hope, encouraged by the signs of the kingdom: healings, expulsion of destructive forces, welcome for the outcasts, meals of camaraderie.

The utopia of the kingdom thus has nothing in common with the sophistication of other utopias, such as Plato's republic or Thomas More's ideal society. These are really *ou-topias*—"places that do not exist"—precisely because of the perfection that they presuppose, and the impossibility of achieving this in the miserable historical realm that is our lot. The utopia of the Gospels—and of liberation theology—is more modest, but more human. It is also more necessary and more urgent: it strives simply to make a just and dignified existence become a reality for poor people, so that the very real cruelty of their sufferings does not have the last word. People who are not poor simply take life for granted, and that gives rise to their fantastic utopias. But life is precisely what poor people do not take for granted. Thus, life itself is the utopia, minimally for the nonpoor, but maximally for the poor. According to Latin American tradition, the poor are those who die before their time, and what they desire is precisely not to die before their time. For that reason we insist upon seeking the *eu-topia*—"the place of the good"—and we insist also that it not be *ou-topia*, a nonexistent place, but *topia*, that which must have a place. We must therefore labor courageously to reverse the current trend and change our death-dealing reality into a life-giving reality.

The poor are the oppressed. They are deprived of life and livelihood. Their death is therefore not only a negation of life, but also a negation of fraternity. Conversely, the overcoming of such inflicted death is the condition not only of "life for all," but of "life communion of all." However, this is not just any nominal, diluted type of fraternity—even though some seek to trace its roots back to the Enlightenment and the French Revolution or to make us believe it is coextensive with democracy; rather it is the fraternity that is expressed in the praxis of overcoming the death of poor people—and of course in not causing such death. In this way universal fraternity can be a way of giving formulation to the universal utopia.

Behind this vision of utopia—from among the poor—there is a particular experience of God. God sees the suffering of poor people, hears their cries, and, through historical signs, defends and loves them (and in that order), as Puebla affirms (no. 1142). Only then does God's glory shine forth so that we can see it. Such is the emphasis of two well-known phrases. The first is one we already cited from J. B. Metz: *sub specie contrarii.* "From being a religion sensitive to suffering, Christianity became ever more a religion sensitive to sin."[3] Our intention here is not to trivialize sin, but to make suffering the main focus, that on which God directly places his gaze and his heart (for which reason Jesus turns toward and welcomes those who suffer). This can be applied to all human beings, but quite especially to the poor. The other phrase is that of Archbishop Romero: *gloria Dei vivens pauper,*[4] "the glory of God is the poor person fully alive." God's glory, then, is not just a matter of anything at all; it refers to those who are without life attaining life.

The hope for that utopia thrives on the signs of the kingdom, liberating signs like those of Jesus, but it thrives most decisively on signs of love. Hope is not a product of extrapolations, calculations, or optimism, as important as these may be for other reasons. And it is hope against hope. It thrives on the love of those who commit themselves in solidarity with the poor and who generously offer their lives for the sake of the poor. From this arises the central paradox of Christianity: a cross, for the sake of love, is announced as that which generates hope. We will return to that theme in addressing how the announcement of the kingdom leads to the cross, but it is important to make this clear from the start. Whether it is called "justification," "salvation," "redemption," "true life," or "eternal life," it happens through God's love revealed in the cross of Jesus.

Announcing the utopia of life by generating hope in credible ways, by means of signs and pledges, is the very first thing—in our view—that the kingdom of God keeps demanding today of Christians and of the Churches. And if, whether by action or omission, we do not do this, perhaps we will have to hear pronounced against us the words of Scripture: "Because of you God's name is blasphemed among the nations."

The Anti-Kingdom

What negates the utopia is not its absence, or its "not-yet" aspect, but the active presence of the sin of the world, which configures the world as an anti-kingdom, as the "certainly-not." Previously we stated that "sin is that which deals death": it is what dealt death to the Son of God and what continues to deal death to the sons and daughters of God. Such language is little used nowadays. Perhaps there are sufficient laments about the evils that exist in the world, but vigorous condemnations are few, and effective commitments to eradicate them are practically nonexistent—especially if such commitment should carry risks or lower one's standard of living. However, to know the shape of the kingdom today and, above all, to know what we must struggle against to promote the kingdom, we have to become very familiar with the shape of the anti-kingdom. Among the thousands of facts about the reality of our planet, we recall a few that are especially applicable to our continent:

> There is more wealth on Earth, but also more injustice. Africa has been called the world's "dungeon," a continental *Shoah*. Some 2.5 billion people survive on Earth with less than two Euros a day, and 25,000 persons die daily of hunger, according to the FAO. Desertification threatens the life of 1.2 billion people in some one hundred countries. . . . Immigrants are denied fraternity, and even the ground beneath their feet. The United States is building a 1,500-kilometer wall against Latin America, while Europe is raising up a barrier against Africa in southern Spain. All of this, besides being iniquitous, is programmed. —Bishop Pedro Casaldáliga

A Dehumanized World: Insensitivity and Cruelty

In the time of Jesus, people were convinced that the world was dominated by malevolent forces—demons—that produced physical and psychic evils and that terrorized and enslaved human beings. Jesus did not deny the existence of such forces; in a way, he radicalized them by uniting them into a single force, Beelzebub, the power of evil. Besides these demonic forces, Jesus also exposed other malevolent, historical forces: quite visible, namable, belligerent forces that took concrete form in the human groups that held power.

Somewhat anachronistically, the Gospels indict the arrogant Pharisees for their (hypocritical) power in proposing themselves as models. More historically, the same Gospels indict the scribes for their intellectual power. And even more clearly they indict the high priests for their religious power (at that time, the most decisive of all), which was joined to their political power (they made the major decisions about Israel as a nation), their economic power (revolving in large part around the temple), their financial power (they coined currency), and their sociocultural power (they established norms that determined the worthiness or unworthiness of citizens).

What is important is the conclusion: with their oppressive power, these forces configure the world as an anti-kingdom. The reality within which Jesus announces the kingdom is not, then, a tabula rasa; it is a force that is actively opposed to the kingdom. His vision of reality is dialectic, and his praxis cannot consist only in beneficence, but must, for all the reasons mentioned, consist also in liberation. The consequence for today continues to be important: the praxis of persons and the Churches can and should be beneficent (the charity of Mother Teresa, for example). But that is not enough; the praxis must also be liberating (the justice of Archbishop Romero, for example)—and thus arises the need for a theology of liberation for understanding Christianity. Moreover, we should not forget that beneficence may well produce suffering, though not necessarily persecution, while liberation will certainly produce both. Both types of praxis can generate credibility, but the second, directly confronting the anti-kingdom, generates a specific credibility, as in the case of Jesus and Romero.

Let us go a step further. The relation between the kingdom and the anti-kingdom is not only dialectic, but dual: one acts against the other. This point must be well understood, because the forces and the operating modes of the two realms are quite different. That the anti-kingdom acts against the kingdom—the world of the oppressors and the wealthy against the world of the oppressed and the poor—is quite evident. We must, however, also explain how the kingdom, by its nature, acts against the anti-kingdom, that is, how the world of the poor acts against the world of the wealthy. This explanation is especially necessary when liberation movements arise.

There are legitimate ways for the poor to struggle against the anti-kingdom—as, for example, in social organizations and grassroots movements—but we must also keep in mind the need for appropriate modes of resistance and be aware of the dangers of dehumanization that are involved in every struggle. There is, however, something quite specific that we need take into account, namely, that the poor and the impoverished, just by what they are, are already acting against the anti-kingdom, by virtue of their potential for exposing it for what it is. In the poor, reality itself raises its voice, whether in the form of cries ("the salary you have not paid to the workers cries out to the Lord" [James 5:4]), or laments ("how will I sing to the Lord in a strange land?" [Ps. 137:4]), or pleas for assistance ("Lord, have mercy on me"), or simply longings ("they shall not hurt or destroy in all my holy mountain" [Isa. 65:25]). Most clearly of all, reality raises its voice in the form of truth: poverty exposes the blindness, the cover-up, the need to awaken from the dogmatic dream of a cruel inhumanity; as Montesinos used to say in Hispañola: "How can they stay so long asleep in lethargic slumber?" Sometimes the voice takes the form of forgiveness, whereby the victims, unarmed, can disarm the executioners. When we understand the kingdom and its relation to the anti-kingdom, we understand the dual dimension of reality and the asymmetry between the forms of struggle, something that the powerful try to conceal by every means possible. We return to this point later.

We make one final observation about the anti-kingdom. Today there exist tremendous and unprecedented possibilities for knowing the reality of our world just as it is, with all that it has in it of anti-kingdom and all the deaths it produces. As experience demonstrates, however, to know the world truly and to allow oneself to be affected by it, simple access to data is not sufficient, as abundant and trustworthy as the data may be, including those of the UNDP. Serious analyses are not sufficient either, nor are truthful testimonies, as important as all these may be for other reasons. The reality of the anti-kingdom, its magnitude and its cruelty, can be truly grasped only by experiencing it *in actu*, in action, when it is actually dealing death. That is what is capable of moving people not only to laments, but to the struggle against the anti-kingdom.

Finally, if we use the terminology of the "anti-kingdom of God," rather than speak of "evils" and "misfortunes," we do so consciously, in order to bestow theologal status once again on the world's evil. The fact that in Africa people can buy food products coming from the United States at lower prices than they can buy their own products, since the former are subsidized, is a "crime against God" that cries out to heaven. The fact that hunger is caused not just by climatic catastrophes, but by the food policies of profit-making multinational businesses with no concern for the lives of millions of destitute people, renders obsolete the customary language of people "dying of hunger"; rather we need to say, "they are being killing by hunger." It is a crime against God.

God of Life and Idols of Death

The kingdom is of God, and the anti-kingdom has its own divinities. Let us therefore reflect on the God of the kingdom and on faith in him, which, again, is in dialectic and dual relationship with the divinities of the anti-kingdom and the idolatry that they require.

A few years ago this topic was fundamental. Juan Luis Segundo used to say that, existentially speaking, the most pressing problem was not that of faith and atheism, but that of faith and idolatry. And with the help of exegetes (von Rad, José Luis Sicre), a new definition of idols emerged: historical realities that promise salvation. To that end they require a cult and an orthodoxy, and above all, like Moloch, they require victims in order to subsist. The conclusion is of the greatest importance: there exists a transcendental correlation between idols and victims. Where there are victims, there are also idols. Idolatry, therefore, finds expression not principally in the religious realm, but in history itself. The astonishing thing is that such idolatry is today a characteristic not of "primitive peoples," but most especially of "civilized peoples."

Puebla mentions idols frequently (nos. 405, 491, 493, 497, and 500), and it concentrates them hierarchically in wealth (nos. 493–97) and political power (nos. 498–506); those are the idols that cause the most victims. Archbishop Romero did the same in his fourth pastoral letter, in 1979. Among the idols are the absolutizing of three concepts: wealth, private property, and national security. The absolutizing of popular organization can also be considered an idol. Romero saw grassroots organization as good and necessary in itself, and for that reason he defended and accompanied the organizations. When they were absolutized, however, they could turn into idols, and whenever he saw that happen, he criticized and denounced them.

There is not much talk these days of idols. With a kind of transcendental redundancy, there is a vague insistence that any created thing, when absolutized, can become an idol. While this is true, it usually does not go beyond being a sterile tautology. Usually the idols are not associated at all with the unconcealable victims of hunger and of arms (the first more numerous now than ever), all slaughtered with immense cruelty. We must return, then, to Puebla and its condemnation of idols, keeping in mind three points.

The first is a pastoral matter and is of great importance. Many people talk these days of growing secularization and agnosticism, and it is quite true that such phenomena exist. However, there is little sensible discussion of why they exist: the Churches and individual Christians are all too easily freed of blame. Yet it would seem that the specific denial of the theologal reality consists precisely in that, and the result is that idolatry is overlooked as original and originating theologal sin.

The second point is historical. A certain unification of idols has taken place today; they have taken on the form of empire, specifically the U.S. empire. The facts are clear, and so is the underlying ideology: in the war between the two superpowers, the United States and the Soviet Union, the former emerged triumphant and so earned the right to an empire—besides having justified it religiously as "manifest destiny," above all in the Bush administration. Be that as it may, the empire is an idol at a planetary level and continues to be, as St. Augustine used to say, *magnum latrocinium*. This point should not be overlooked, either in theology or in the judgment of the Churches.

Of course, other societies and other civilizations are seriously tainted by idolatry as well, certainly insofar as they willingly keep themselves within the orbit of the empire and thrive on it: they enjoy the goods produced by it, and they do not seriously oppose it in the name of any ideal, divine or human, religious or democratic. Also within their borders they perform idolatrous actions that produce victims either by omission or by commission; either they facilitate the idolatry or they do nothing to impede it. Although there are some exceptions, even important ones, one need only recall the ignorance, for the most part culpable, of the West, of the whole of it, concerning the suffering of the Third World and its causes—and to recall its insensibility before the "wretched living" or the "cruel dying" of the destitute world, on which the "good living" of the West is in good measure based.

Globalization does not improve the situation; rather, it often makes it worse. What we must insist on, however, is that globalization most definitely and of necessity, and not just accidentally, produces victims. As an economic reality, which it is basically, "It has produced winners and losers, beneficiaries and victims," according to economist Luis de Sebastián. The conclusion is that, in order to believe truly in the God of the kingdom, one must be actively atheistic with regard to the gods of the empire, and one's faith should be actively anti-idolatrous.

The third point is a recent phenomenon, one more specifically European, though it also reaches our shores: the return of the idols. Postmodernity values this return of the idols, in the plural; the return may result from disenchantment, but is definitely seen as positive. The reason is that, in contrast to the monotheistic gods, who along with their adorers are in conflict with one another, the gods of polytheism get along well together, and they make pluralism and coexistence easier. For that reason some people intone a hymn of praise to the idols.[5]

Such theologal irenicism is convenient for the West's welfare and is understandably desired in the face of the actions of Islamic groups—and of every monotheistic religion, in the opinion of some. Such irenicism offers advantages, but it is not an answer to the profound ills of our reality. "Several" gods, pacifist ones, are enthroned in order to get rid of the "one and only" God, whose essence is to bring about justice. Thus, sanction is given to a pluralistic reality, though one that is fallaciously homogeneous, since it has been stripped of its fundamental contours. In this way, what is "other" can easily disappear, and most certainly "the other" who is "the poor person," who ends up being just "one more." In this way, heaven itself takes the edge off the horrible differences (the rich man and Lazarus) and the cruel oppositions (victims and executioners) that exist on earth.[6]

The praise of polytheism may be able to overcome, conceptually, the evils of the violent struggle among the monotheistic gods, but it leaves the victims without a God—at least Jesus' God—who defends them. It does away with the dialectic of some gods against others, but it also does away with the challenging, questioning, and enabling otherness; it causes "the other" to disappear—above all "the poor other," the one that unsettles us, challenges us, and offers us salvation. This loss is irreparable.

The Centrality of the Poor in Christianity

"The poor will have the good news announced to them" (Luke 4:18), proclaims Jesus in the synagogue of Nazareth. In a much cited text, J. Jeremias comments: "The kingdom belongs *only* to the poor."[7] If this is so, then "kingdom of God" and "poor people" are correlatives. To speak of the "kingdom" without focusing on the "poor" is impossible, which in turn means that no Jesuanic Christianity is possible if the poor are not at its center.

We already mentioned the poor in an earlier section. We wish now to probe deeper into just two points that are fundamental for the Churches' self-understanding and mission. We shall do this quite briefly, since the second and third chapters of this book treat the same matter. The first point concerns the "option for the poor," a central theme for Medellín, for liberation theology, and for the life and death of communities—and we recall it because this option is extremely difficult to maintain. The second point is more novel and provocative: accepting that "salvation comes from the poor." Both theses are difficult to accept, but the second gives more problems than the first. Whatever the difficulties, however, two realities are undeniable: the poor are the immense majority of humankind, and the poor are at the center of the Gospels.

Many advances have been made in developing the concept of "poverty" beyond its socioeconomic meaning, which might be more correctly described as the "primary dimension of life." That was the basic significance of poverty, though not the only one, at the beginnings of liberation theology. The option for the poor, since it is God's own option, is unappealable, but it is difficult. For that reason we are going to focus now not on its contents, but on the very fact of the option and on the decision to maintain it—or return to it. What needs to be stressed is the depth of this option. It is a question of placing the poor at the center of Christianity, using whatever analogies may be needed.

Let us recall that placing the poor at the center does not happen in the world of democracy, certainly not in reality, but not even theoretically; I don't know how much it happened in socialism or at what cost. Neither does it happen in the Church. Despite the desires of John XXIII, Cardinal Lercaro, and Bishop Himmer (*primus locus in Ecclesia pauperibus reservandus est*), the Church of the poor had no real success in the Second Vatican Council.

As regards the Church, the difficulty of the option is first of all theoretical, because of the intellectual mortgages, more or less bourgeois and not very biblical, taken on by theologies in the course of history. The difficulty is also practical, since, as was the case for Jesus, the option for the poor leads to persecution, defamation, a feeling of being abandoned by old friends. . . . Not only that, but if we radicalize the concept, we can say that even God can be an "object of intellectual persecution" precisely because of his option. Regarding a God who makes an option for the poor there is a theoretical problem of theodicy: how do we accept the existence of God, and precisely of a God who favors the poor, when cruel injustice oppresses them so mercilessly? The suffering and death of the poor have made the question of theodicy problematic from ancient times: "According to a very real Christian tradition, but one that has been carefully forgotten, the greatest argument against the existence of God is the existence of poor people" (J. I. González Faus). The question takes on new life in liberation theology, where poor people are taken as seriously as is God: "God the Father ended up with many poor children. . . . The problem of the poor is the problem of God" (I. Ellacuría). Drawing close to the poor, especially when making an option for them, can lead to a serious posing of the eternal, painful question: "Lord, why have you abandoned them? Why have you abandoned the peasants, the native peoples, the malnourished children, the AIDS patients without means?"

And the difficulty is obviously a practical one as well. Puebla formulates the option for the poor, in its theologal dimension, in this way: "God takes up the defense [of poor people] and he loves them" (no.

1142). We can readily accept that God loves the poor, unconditionally, even if such love is difficult to imitate. But his defense of the poor supposes the introduction of inevitable conflict into the very concept of the option, since in real-life history it is impossible to defend somebody without in some way confronting and opposing those who are trying to harm.

If in real life the option for the poor means not only loving but also defending the poor, we should not wonder that persecution will arise. We may seek to disregard the persecution or assuage it, but it is inevitable, for it has a theologal basis. History gives many examples of the option watered down with a thousand qualifications. One way of doing so is with adjectives: the option for the poor is said to be "preferential," but not "exclusive" or "exclusionary." Though this qualification has something positive to it ("We must love everybody"), such a reminder should be unnecessary, since the people who have most brilliantly practiced the option for the poor, from Jesus down to Romero, never excluded anybody.

It therefore makes you wonder at the insistence on placing so many "additions" onto the option. As we have said before, it personally reminds me of the end of Mark's Gospel: something similar, I believe, could happen, either consciously or unconsciously, with the option for the poor. Of course, the modifier "preferential" is "orthodox," just as the present end of Mark's Gospel is "canonical"—though one may doubt whether it is "logical." The option for the poor is costly and is never *in possessione*. If taken seriously, it is very demanding, and there always arises an urge to moderate and soften it. The lesson remains: maintaining the depth of that option is difficult. Nonetheless, the option for the poor is *articulus stantis vel cadentis ecclesiae*. And to that option the Church must return in Aparecida, with no illusions about its being something already known, understood, accepted, or seriously practiced.

The profundity of the option is even more astonishing when it has to do with "letting ourselves be saved by the poor," as we have seen.

The Following of Jesus

Whenever Christianity has been in crisis, the most lucid minds have turned to Jesus of Nazareth and, specifically, to following him. We must avoid the Christological reductionism, or Christomonism, which is usually considered responsible for the dangers inherent in voluntarism, fanaticism, and spiritless law—though I believe that the opposite phenomena could be even more dangerous. Most certainly, Jesus is the one who saves Christianity, and the following of Jesus is what makes us Christians. The Spirit is the force of God that makes us truly become "followers," "sons in the Son." Francis of Assisi and Ignatius of Loyola saw this with total clarity. Today it is equally necessary to see it so.

As regards the concern of this essay for the themes to be treated in Aparecida, we should recall that, immediately after his programmatic announcement of the kingdom, Jesus calls for followers (he afterward calls women by name). He calls them to be with him, to be sent by him, and, as the end approaches, to participate in his destiny. All of this is heard in his lapidary "Follow me"—the first and final word of Jesus to Peter, as Bonhoeffer used to say.[8] The following of Jesus is the specifically Christian way of responding to God's passing through this world, and of contributing to his reign.

Following and Praxis: "Assuming Responsibility for the Kingdom"

Ellacuría used to say, "The greatest possible realization of the kingdom of God in history [the very thing that Jesus came to announce and bring about] is what the true followers of Jesus must pursue."[9] Historical adjustments obviously need to be made as regards the contents and attitudes of this following, but we wish to insist now on the following as such, as a kind of praxis in which we "assume responsibility for the kingdom of God." We must do so without falling into either hubris or Pelagianism (excessive "activism," to use popular language). Even more important, though, it seems to us, is not falling into irresponsibility, even for virtuous reasons: we should not delegate to others, not even (just) to God, the task of making the world human. Let us try to explain.

First of all, praxis and grace are not opposed; rather, construction of the kingdom and gift of God converge—or they might well converge. More useful than conceptual arguments for demonstrating this is to look at what happens in history. We might begin with the life of Paul, paladin at once of both grace and praxis, although in his case, rather than speak of construction of the kingdom in the style of Jesus, we would better speak of construction of communities with the values of Jesus. In history there is grace: Christians have received "new" ears for hearing the word which is from God (the faith that comes to us by hearing) and "new" eyes for seeing God in the poor, in the Risen One (the Greek *ophthe*, "he let himself be seen," of the apparition narratives). And history shows equally, and just as vigorously, that there are

Christians who have also received "new" hands for building the kingdom, and that also is grace.

We cite frequently these words of Archbishop Romero: "With this people it is not difficult to be a good pastor." By so quoting him, we wish to point out his experience of grace, which he attributed ultimately to God. But he continues: "This is a people that pushes us to serve," to "defend their rights," and "to be their voice" (Homily of November 18, 1979). And that is praxis, "assuming responsibility for the kingdom." In the following of Jesus it is necessary to insist on both things, praxis and grace, or better still, on praxis replete with grace—and among ourselves we should recall that we are pushed towards praxis by "others," specifically by the poor and their advocates, like Romero. Nowadays, certainly, we must insist especially on praxis, in order to overcome the infantilism which, more than the activisms of the past, is what most proliferates in our time. "The Christian faith itself is being made into a recipe book of miracles and prosperity, into a spiritualist refuge in the face of evil and suffering, and into a substitute for personal and communitarian co-responsibility in the transformation of society."[10]

Even less should there be an opposition between praxis and spirit, as long as this latter is understood as *spiritus*, *pneuma*, all that is wind, force, energy, all that is related with a being and a doing; "spirit" should not be understood as a vaporous reality that moves about invisibly and immaterially and that produces a sort of "spirituality for its own sake." Those who dedicate themselves to "constructing" the kingdom of God know this well. Without spirit it is impossible to work for truth, justice, fraternity, peace, or reconciliation. We must insist here that the Spirit is the one who comes from the Father and from the Son, from Jesus (to paraphrase the *filioque*); it is not just any spirit, and even less is it a spirit apart from or over against Jesus. It is the spirit of the Beatitudes and the Sermon on the Mount; it is the spirit that is expressed in the lucid recognition of what is new and in the audacious response to its exigencies. Perhaps most difficult, it is the spirit that takes us out of and frees us from ourselves. It is the spirit that enables us to call upon God both as "God," that is, radical otherness, and simultaneously as "Father," that is, maximum nearness. The Spirit is working in us when we can, at one and the same time, place our trust and take our repose in God and yet not be able to rest in the presence of God, the unmanipulable one.

This Spirit remits us back to the concrete Jesus, but it does not close off any spirit of God that is present in other religions and cultures. Even historically, it is possible to demonstrate a universalism that characterizes the spirit of Jesus. Gandhi made the Beatitudes central to his praxis.

Today, when Christianity should open up to everybody and should co-operate with all those who desire to construct truth, justice, and peace, it may well be that the spirit of the Beatitudes, as preached and lived by Jesus, provides the concrete springboard and trampoline by which we open ourselves to the Spirit of the infinite God, which blows where it will.

To sum up: praxis without spirit is a grave danger, but so too—and I believe today with even worse consequences—is spirit without praxis. Spirituality should empower and cleanse praxis, but praxis should not be moderated in the name of spirituality, lest spirituality itself be lost, nor should Christianity be infantilized. Jesus did not act that way. And the world is not for running such risks.

The Following and Martyrdom: "Bearing the Weight of the Anti-Kingdom"

The tradition has always stressed how costly the following of Jesus is. At times, because of the influence of a pain-centered religiosity, it has made imitation of Christ and suffering to coincide. In the Gospels, how-ever, what is specifically costly in following Christ comes from the praxis of announcing the good news of God, of building the kingdom and of confronting the anti-kingdom. In Mark's Gospel, right from the start Jesus became involved in serious conflicts precisely for acting on behalf of the kingdom. He healed in the synagogue on a Sabbath, and "the Pharisees went out and immediately held counsel with the Herodians against him, to see how to destroy him" (Mark 3.6). It was the begin-ning of a persecution that finally led to his crucifixion, not because of a misunderstanding (as Bultmann claimed), but because he was confront-ing the anti-kingdom head-on. The cross, in its concrete reality of cru-elty and death, need not be, obviously, the fate of all those who work for the kingdom, but—to some degree and analogously—it is inherent in every attempt to follow Jesus.

In our own setting, this concept is something understood by even the simplest of poor farmers. All those who have resembled Jesus and have followed him, all those who have worked for justice, truth, and the dignity of the oppressed, have been persecuted and even killed. The praxis of the kingdom disturbs the mighty ones, and as Archbishop Romero used to say, "Whoever disturbs is killed." We insist on this because some people say—or like to think—that recalling this is a form of impenitent, unpardonable, irresponsible masochism; at the very least they will think it to be an anachronism. But the thesis is still valid: whoever assumes responsibility for the kingdom must be ready to bear the weight of the anti-kingdom. Refusing to see it this way is ingenuous and self-deceiving, and it is a great danger for Christians and for the Churches. None of this changes with globalization.

Understandably, the epochs when there is "peace for the Church" are always longed for and welcomed; it is one of the most repeated liturgical prayers, as it was in the time of Constantine. Nonetheless, we must take great care not to make such peace the basic criterion of how well Christianity is doing; even less should we justify peace simply because it allows the Church to evangelize better. To be sure, we must work for peace and rejoice in it, but we must do so while ever relating the peace of the Church with the peace of the oppressed world, the peace longed for by the peoples who suffer misery and violence; we must do so without absolutizing peace, as if it were the greatest good that could happen for Christians and the most beneficial gift for the Churches. We must remember that without justice—which is central in the construction of the kingdom—there can be no peace. In other words, we say yes to shalom, peace with justice, the life of poor people (wherein the Church lives). But as long as we live in an anti-kingdom world, we consider dangerous both the *pax romana*, a product of stipulated agreements (with the Church), and the Greek *eirene,* a mere absence of war (for the Church). Situations may change, but the principle must be maintained: "A Church that does not suffer persecution should fear for itself. It is not the true Church of Jesus Christ," stated Archbishop Romero. And we should not forget, but rather should be very aware, that any persecution that arises for those same reasons for which they persecuted Jesus is always an a posteriori verification, and probably the most powerful one, that Christianity has in fact existed. These words are strong but eloquent ones, and they allow no mitigation.

This point is fundamental. Many Christians, and many other human beings, have been killed for "assuming responsibility for the kingdom," and thus have they "borne the weight of the anti-kingdom." Whatever may be the canonical precisions necessary concerning those we call "Jesuanic martyrs" (the people call them simply "martyrs"), our not remembering them is an ingratitude that dehumanizes us as human beings and impoverishes us as Christians. In some truly analogous sense, we who are believers today live by those martyrs, as we live by Christ crucified (and therefore risen). Those followers of Jesus up to the very end are the best that the Church of these years has produced. They have molded it as the true Church of Jesus. They have introduced truth into a world of lies, and compassion into a world of insensibility and cruelty. By Christian paradox, they have introduced life into a world of death.

Ignoring them is to direct the Church along a road that is mistaken, impoverishing, non-Christian, or even anti-Christian.

In this context it is important to call to mind those whom we call the Holy Fathers of Latin America, that Pleiades of bishops around Medellín and Puebla who brought about the convergence within the people of God—then very creative and very persecuted—of the hierarchy and the rest of the baptized. They were true pastors, but they also lived under constant threat and persecution without letting themselves be intimidated, and often even in the Church they were marginalized. Some of them were murdered, such as Enrique Angelelli in Argentina, Oscar Romero (and later Joaquín Ramos, in 1993) in El Salvador, and Juan Gerardi in Guatemala. Others were imprisoned. The most notable symbolic event was the imprisonment of seventeen bishops in Riobamba, Ecuador, in 1976. They are eloquent symbols of a Church that in its totality—hierarchy, laity, religious, priests, Christian *campesinos* and professionals—bears the weight of the anti-kingdom.

Last, if we are to speak decisively of "bearing the weight of reality," we must remember all those millions of poor people who are persecuted, who are slowly but relentlessly oppressed by injustice and who are often violently repressed. They die in the most absolute anonymity, but they are the crucified people, the suffering servant of Yahweh. They are not followers of Jesus according to the concept we have just spelled out, but they bear a profound resemblance to Jesus, in many cases even greater than that of the Jesuanic followers: they resemble Jesus poor and overwhelmed. As we have written elsewhere, these people possess a primordial holiness. They are the favored ones of God, and of them is the kingdom. For that reason we must give them a central place in Christianity and in the Churches. Ignoring them while talking about the following of Jesus would be theological ineptitude, but even worse, it would be impoverishment and ingratitude.

The Following and Transcendence: "Letting Ourselves Be Borne toward God"

Faith is oriented toward transcendence. Let us end this essay by saying a very brief word about how the following of Jesus—for the sake of the kingdom—can illuminate faith. And we speak of grace, of "letting ourselves be carried," since real access to transcendence is certainly always replete with grace.

A word about the transcendence of Christ. We have spoken of the kingdom of God announced by Jesus, and we confess Jesus to be the Christ.

That is definitely a leap of faith, something that can't be programmed. And if we ask what makes the leap reasonable, the answer can only be the true following of Jesus. Some time ago we expressed it this way:

> Having access to Christ always supposes some type of discontinuity, but . . . such access is possible, ultimately, only on the basis of some type of continuity between Jesus and those who know him; and that continuity should be conceived from the spot where reality has its maximum density, which in our vision is practice with spirit. Accordingly, having access to Jesus is not, first of all, a matter of knowing about him, or of developing a hermeneutic that makes knowledge about Jesus possible but preserves the distance between him and us. Rather, it is ultimately a matter of affinity and connaturality, beginning with what is most real in Jesus. . . . Following Jesus in his practice with spirit is, then, an ethical exigency of the historical Jesus himself, but it is also an epistemological principle. . . . To give it a negative formulation: apart from the following of Jesus, there can never be affinity with the object of faith that is sufficient for knowing what is being said in confessing him to be the Christ. Expressing it positively: it can make sense, on the basis of the affinity of the following, to proclaim Jesus to be the Christ, to be the revelation of the truly divine and the truly human.[11]

Simply put, the following of Jesus gives us an experience of whether the mystery of reality yields more "yes" or more "no," of whether hope is more sensible than disenchantment, of whether self-giving until the very end is better than the carpe diem, and of whether the life of Jesus, "lived for us," opens up forever onto more life, without limit, and is blessed.

A word about the transcendence of God. The formula "following Jesus" corresponds to the Old Testament formula "walking with God": we do justice, love tenderly, and walk humbly with God (Micah 6:8). Well then, the following of Jesus for the sake of the kingdom helps us to describe how we now must walk: *building the kingdom and bearing with the anti-kingdom.* Thus do we walk in history with a God-Father, and we make our way toward absolute mystery. As we "assume responsibility for the kingdom of God," that mystery can appear above all as *abba*, as the beloved nearness in which Jesus trusts. As we "bear with the anti-kingdom," the mystery can appear above all as God, the one beyond manipulation, for whom Jesus is available.

In the following of Jesus we can make our own that same experience of the God-Father that Jesus had, and the following guarantees that such experience will contain the two fundamental elements of the mystery of God: "being Father" and "still being God." Maintaining both aspects dialectically makes the experience a process, which it has to be, as it was for Jesus. It is "walking" with God in justice, love, and tenderness, and it is walking toward God without ever attaining possession of him.

The following of Jesus can also forcefully raise the question of theodicy: why is there so much cruelty against the poor?—a question asked even by great believers. And there can appear an answer, in praxis: by walking "with God" in history, more can come out of that history. The poor can remain committed to life, they can maintain their hope, and keep on walking.

In the end, the experience of transcendence cannot be programmed, but that does not render superfluous the question about a privileged place in history for such experience. Years ago Porfirio Miranda[12] used to say, "The problem is not in seeking God, but in seeking him where he said he was"—and he explained: in the poor people of this world. And we might add that the problem also is in "seeking him as he wanted us to seek him"—and we might explain: in the following of Jesus. When we assume the following of Christ, the following takes us to God. In a similar context Karl Rahner wrote at the end of his life:

> I believe that being Christian is the easiest and simplest task, and at the same time it is that light burden of which the gospel speaks. When you bear the burden, the burden bears you, and the longer you live the heavier and the lighter it will become. At the end there remains only the mystery. But it is the mystery of Jesus.[13]

A Final Word

The three reflections we have offered on utopia, the poor, and the following of Jesus from the perspective of the kingdom of God need to be analyzed in more depth. May these reflections serve to call attention to the matter and to stimulate the proceedings of the Aparecida conference. We could add several further reflections, but we mention here only a few of them:

1. *Understanding and analyzing the concept "people of God" in relation to that of the kingdom of God.* This is a relationship more basic

than that with the Church (Ellacuría), though it is obviously urgent that its supremacy be recovered within the Church, according to chapter 2 of *Lumen Gentium.*

2. *Configuration of the internal ecclesial levels within the Church (the ministries), not only on the basis of the legitimate ecclesial norms that have developed in the course of history, and not even only on the basis of Jesus' words, whether historical or attributed to him in the post-Easter period, but also on the basis of the objective requirements of the construction of the kingdom in the course of history.* In other words, the logic of the kingdom announced by Jesus should direct the logic of the institution, our understanding of the ministries, and our ways of carrying them out.

3. *Making the most fundamental aspects of the kingdom (justice, peace, the centrality of the poor) the minimum/maximum of any ecumenism among Christians, among religions and among human beings.* The a priori presupposition should be that it is possible for all human beings—God's creation—to recognize in those aspects the salvation of humanity, the humanity of the poor majorities. Whether it will prove to be true a posteriori will depend on our dedicating ourselves, in credible fashion, to the work that groups and the Churches will remit to the kingdom, and on its fruits being seen.

Much of what we have said in this essay we have published before, but we repeat it because saying it still seems to us to be necessary. Despite the diversity of social, religious, and ecclesial situations in the different countries of Latin America—in Central America, for example, persecution and martyrdom have shaped what is fundamental in faith, the Church, and theology—our hope is that the reflections we have offered are of some usefulness for the Fifth Bishops' Conference to be held in Aparecida.

—*Translated by Joseph Owens*

5

The Resurrection of One Crucified

Hope and a Way of Living

Death and Victims

Human beings understand death and what comes after it in a variety of ways. This understanding can also shape their lives.

At times they have understood death as the ending of their existence in peace and with a degree of naturalness, and so, in cultures where the nation was considered more important than the individual, as in ancient Israel, they could say "he reached the end of his years and went to be united with his ancestors." At times, as with Christianity, life and fullness are posited after death: "Happy those who die in the Lord."

Overall, though, death remains a negative thing. Many feel the rift of separation with no consolation or resist accepting nothing (Unamuno). Epicurus can bring psychology some comfort: "While you are alive you need not worry, and when you are dead you cannot worry." Or, more solemnly, Socrates before his judges: "Now is the time for us to part, me to death and you to life. Which is better? That is hidden from mortals. Only the divinity knows it."

Today, in prosperous societies, although death is still resisted, there is an increasing tendency not to take death too seriously. It is hushed up, made up. These, and many others, are reactions, if I may say so, to the death of the "dead."

There are, however, other deaths that carry with them an added element of scandal that cannot be grasped by reason or by faith. A major scandal is the death of children who have not lived out their days and

Published in *Concilium* 318 (2006/5): 100–109. Andrés Torres Queiruga, Luiz Carlos Susin, and Jon Sobrino, eds., *The Resurrection of the Dead.*

who have even, in their innocence, been murdered. Ivan Karamazov found no consolation in the idea that children torn to pieces by dogs on the orders of a lieutenant could go to a place in which they would be integrated into a universal harmony: "If they invite me to that heaven, from now on I'll send the invitation back." This is the scandal that has no resolution, and it goes on happening. Children, and also adult and old men and women, are wickedly murdered by national security regimes, or die as "collateral damage," or as a result of perfectly avoidable hunger.[1] This is why from now on we should take the commemoration of the Holy Innocents seriously and not trivialize it as a piece of Christmas decoration.

Another scandal is the death by assassination of those who have worked and struggled for justice: from the prophets of Israel to the innumerable martyrs and fallen of the last thirty years in Latin America. It may be some comfort to know that their deaths have produced life, and that some of them go on living in some form. But the death of "victims" remains a scandal: the best, those who defend the oppressed, are done to death by injustice.

All this is well known, but I repeat it here so as to provide a proper context for the body of this essay. In the Christian tradition the fate of human beings is understood in the light of the fate of Jesus. What we need to be clear about is that Jesus did not end his life "in the fullness of days" but as a "victim,"[2] and that his resurrection did not consist in giving life back to a corpse but in giving justice back to a victim. The central affirmation is then that "the risen one is the crucified one," which is what John's Jesus also insisted on, by appearing as risen displaying his wounds.

This, which is so clear in the New Testament, has not usually been seen as such. And as a result, neither has it been usual to situate Jesus' death in relation to the crucified reality of the victims of history. A blindness, partly culpable, tends to descend over both things. That is what I am trying to overcome in order to understand both Jesus' resurrection and its meaning for today.

I shall go on to reflect on two things: one, more specific, the hope of the victims; the other, more general, Christian existence, here and now in history, in the light of the resurrection: a life in community with the crucified, in order to take them down from the cross, living already as risen, and walking—with humility in the face of the scandal of history— with the God of the poor and the victims. But first a final observation.

I am writing from a place of victims, and I am trying to reflect from their situation, as an irreplaceable hermeneutical tool for understanding the texts that speak of a crucified man raised.[3] But the difficulty is obvious. The present writer and readers are not victims in the sense that the vast majorities of the poor and oppressed of history are. We have no primary experience of what they feel, suffer, and hope. The fact is that "taking life for granted," our situation, is not at all the same thing as "not taking life for granted," theirs. This does not mean that we can understand nothing of their situation, but neither can we presume that, from ours, we can deploy adequate concepts to understand it. And this, in my view, is a basic problem for a theology whose God is, precisely, a God of poor and victims—a problem that becomes unavoidable when speaking of death and resurrection. Therefore it is only riskily and tentatively that we can speak of what the resurrection of Jesus means for them. And, from their situation, we can perhaps speak of our hope.

A Drama in Two Acts

Jesus' fate as death and resurrection was soon universalized. Proclaiming the fact of his death was important for avoiding docetism, but it brought the risk of putting in the shade the fact that he was put to death. Hope in his resurrection was also widespread, but the nature of the event brought the danger of stressing, unilaterally, God's power, putting God's justice in the shade. To avoid these dangers, let us recall the first Christian preaching on the resurrection, even if this has come down to us in stereotyped and already theologized form.

Jesus' resurrection was preached as a drama in two acts: "[This man] . . . you crucified and killed by the hands of those outside the law. But God raised him up, having freed him from death . . ." (Acts 2:23–24; cf. the same pattern in Acts 3:13–15; 4:10; 5:30; 10:39; 13:28). The raising of Jesus is, then, presented as a response by God to the unjust and criminal actions of human beings, as is expressed by the "but." And as it is a response, we need to be conscious of why Jesus was crucified if we are to understand it properly. Not just anyone was resurrected, but Jesus of Nazareth, who proclaimed the kingdom of God to the poor and defended them, who denounced and unmasked oppressors, and who was persecuted by them, condemned to death and executed, and who throughout all this kept his trust in a God who is Father and his openness to the will of a Father who always showed himself as God, ineffable, beyond manipulation. The conclusion the first Christians very soon drew was that Jesus was persecuted and executed like the prophets (1 Thess. 2:15). They also proclaimed him "the holy one," "the just one," "the giver of life," with which the "verisimilitude" of a final fullness is increased, but so is the scandal: that the world eliminates its best.

Resurrection, therefore, means first and foremost doing justice to a victim, not merely giving new life to a corpse, even if this is its logical presupposition. It refers not simply to a death, but to a cross; not simply to dead people, but to victims; not simply to a power, but to a justice.

The Hope of the Victims

Several important considerations follow from the resurrection of a crucified man. I begin my analysis with what strikes me as most fundamental: it introduces hope into history, into human beings, into the collective consciousness, as a sort of historical life experience capable of giving shape to everything. But let us not be hasty: specifically, it is a matter of a hope for the victims. And by "victims" here I mean both the great masses of the poor and oppressed who are put to death slowly and those who are assassinated for denouncing injustice and actively seeking justice.

It is true that the resurrection can be, and has been, used to release hope in a life "beyond" for everyone. But if the person resurrected is a victim, the hope it produces is hope precisely for victims; they can hope for the justice and life that have been denied them in a thousand ways. In the well-known words of Max Horkheimer, speaking in the fullness of his years, we can hope "that the executioner may not triumph over the victim."[4]

This is the plot of the second act of the drama: God raised Jesus, and since then there is hope for the victims. But we need to define this carefully, or the conclusion can seem excessively literalistic as to the content and excessively daring as to the means of coming to express it.

It is not literalistic, however, since it is in line with the hope produced in Israel since the beginning, expressed in faith in a God who was constitutionally on the side of the victims. This is made clear in Exodus. In the Prophets, in order to judge oppressors harshly, God apostrophizes them as "you," a distancing term that is followed by other threats, while he calls the oppressed "my people" (Isaiah, Amos). Jesus, following in the same vein, proclaims the coming of the kingdom uniquely to the poor, as Joachim Jeremias says, telling them specifically that they will "be filled" and "laugh" (Luke 6.21ff.), not so the rich, who will "be hungry" and "mourn and weep" (6:25). This partiality of God's very nature and of his promises, full of compassion and justice, shines out with absolute clarity from the resurrection of Jesus.

The second objection needs to be taken more seriously: the daring in speaking of the hope of the victims, as I have suggested—especially when by "victims" are understood not only individuals who freely decide to fight for justice, but also the poor and oppressed majorities. The "others," these poor, introduce an asymmetry (Levinas) into reality, which cannot be compensated in concept. The conclusion from this is that we nonpoor cannot know with any precision what hope in general, or the more specific hope in relation to death, means for today's victims. Neither do I know if Adorno's lucid (and Christian) statement, "Hope applies only to others, never to oneself," can be applied equally to poor and nonpoor.[5] I do not actually believe that this can be applied to the poor. I rather see them as having full right to hope for themselves—and let us hope they also have hope for the rest of us.

This does not prevent us from being able to say something about what, faced with Jesus' resurrection, the victims think and feel as the great "other" for us: the poor. But, again, let us not be hasty. It is often supposed that it is easy for them to have hope in another life beyond death, because life here is hugely hostile to them, which, according to Marx, would be the condition for making religion possible, and of which the religions took advantage in order to instill fear. But things are not so simple. I am going to quote not authors but a poor woman, who possessed almost nothing and whose sons had been vilely murdered: "A life after death, without sufferings? How splendid!" I do not think she meant, "There will finally be fulfillment" (alluding to Jesus' resurrection, about which she does not understand much), but, "That will be an end to the suffering I have always undergone" (which she does understand, and so she finds the thought of such a future consoling).

I do not think it is possible for us to delve into the depths of the victims. It is easy to get to learn their specific hopes, but what their overall hope, in its fullness, is remains their secret. From the outside, I believe they can find hope in the resurrection of Jesus, who was crucified like them, but not when it is preached as mere "doctrine," only when it is proclaimed as "good news," accompanied by the love and credibility of an Archbishop Romero.

The Hope of Nonvictims

So what of the hope of the nonpoor, the nonvictims? I believe Jesus' resurrection can indeed generate hope for them, for us. But on two conditions. The first has to do with the reality of the nonvictims.[6] The condition is that they participate, even if only analogously, in the reality of the victims, so that their death is, in some way, like that of Jesus, on a cross. I hope the following will serve to illustrate this analogy. When one's own death is not just the product of physical limitations or the wear and tear of looking after oneself, but when it is the outcome of loving dedication to others and to the weakness, poverty, or defenselessness of these others as a result of injustice, then there is a likeness between one's own life and death and Jesus' life and death. Then—and from a Christian point of view only then—one can also share in the hope of resurrection. In short, community in the life and fate of Jesus is what gives us hope of what was produced in Jesus being produced in us.

Outside this communion with the crucified—Jesus and the victims— however analogous it may be, resurrection only spells out hope of life after death. And according to the most classical doctrine, this possibility does not necessarily generate hope, since it can bring salvation or condemnation. For resurrection to be salvation, the condition is to "die in a state of grace." For it to generate hope, the condition is "to die on the cross," reproducing—to a greater or lesser extent, of course—the life, mission, and fate of Jesus, in trust and availability to a God-Father to the end.

The second has to do with our subjectivity: how is it possible to overcome the scandal of death, which seems to put an end to all hope, whether we are poor or nonpoor? The response is inescapably personal. But we can suggest a way: to face up to the greater scandal of the injustice that already brings death to the victims and try to conquer it through our life choices.

The first condition means that the resurrection of a crucified person should challenge us not only with how we approach not only our own future death, but also with how we, in the here and now, approach the death and life of others. The second is the question of what we ourselves can do to give the victims hope.

With regard to the first condition applied to the nonpoor, the evangelical precept of forgetting oneself to regain oneself—losing one's life to save it—is still valid. Those for whom their own death is the greatest scandal and their hope in an afterlife their main preoccupation will not have a Christian hope or one stemming from Jesus' resurrection.

And with regard to the second, forgetting oneself has to go hand in hand with remembering the victims, which leads to losing one's life for them, doing the opposite of what the victim-makers do. A determined, persevering struggle on behalf of the victims will not produce hope in us mechanically, but it can produce it. It is true that whenever there is true love, hope springs up. "Not all life is an occasion of hope," says

Moltmann, "but the life of Jesus, who took the cross upon himself out of love, is." Wherever there is love, the poor can have hope, and we can have it with them.

Living in Accordance with Jesus' Resurrection

Jesus' resurrection is discussed in various contexts in the New Testament. Up to this point I have concentrated on hope, which can well serve as a judgment around which what it means to be human revolves—which is rather, I think, what Bloch meant in *The Hope Principle*. Let me now add, briefly, other aspects surrounding Jesus' resurrection, which can, together with hope, mold a way of living as human beings and as Christians.

"The Wounds of the Exalted One": Living as though Already Risen in History

In the resurrection, Jesus is exalted. He lives in fullness, but he keeps his wounds. Taking this the other way round, we might say that we live in the wounds of history, but we can also share in fullness. So let us now see how we can live as risen beings in history.

The concept is not new. The Christians of Corinth, surrounded by extraordinary signs—miracles, gifts of tongues, ecstasies—thought they were already living in the resurrection, and they did not even believe in the final resurrection. They came to curse Jesus, and Paul had to rebuke them: "No one speaking by the Spirit ever says, 'Let Jesus be cursed' " (1 Cor. 12:3). Another somewhat closer example: in seminaries and convents the superiority of celibacy over other ways of life used to be justified on the grounds that it allowed a present sharing in the fullness of resurrection, by distancing us from the material conditions of existence and bringing us closer to celestial ones.

The idea is mistaken and dangerous but not totally crazy, since it would be absurd for Jesus to live in fullness and for nothing of this to be reflected back on us. The important thing is to know how we can already live as risen beings and under what conditions. I believe that, for this to come about, we need to live in history something of "fullness" and of "triumph," something that savors of an impossibility become real. Fullness always consists in love, and triumph in overcoming egoism. Let us look at this in three ways.

The first is a life in *freedom that overcomes self-centeredness.* Freedom expresses "fullness" when it introduces us into history in order to "love," and it expresses "triumph" when "nothing is an obstacle" to it. Freedom is then—paradoxically put—binding oneself to history in order to save it. This is what, speaking of himself as a victim, John's Jesus says: "No one takes [my life] from me, but I lay it down of my own accord" (John 10:18). This is the freedom with which an Archbishop Romero lived: he loved the poor and loved nothing more than them (fullness); he allowed no fear to hold him back from any risk (triumph).

The second is the *joy that overcomes sadness*. In situations of great suffering it may seem stupid to speak of joy, but it is possible, and even necessary, and it is found in communities of the poor. They come together to sing and celebrate, to express the joy of being together (fullness). And they can do this because, as Gustavo Gutiérrez once heard said in a community of poor people, "The opposite of joy is not suffering but sadness. We suffer, but we are not sad" (triumph). In the midst of a thousand problems, Oscar Romero used to say, "It's not hard to be a good shepherd to this people."

The third is *the justice and love needed to "take the crucified down from the cross."* Here we are facing an extreme case of analogy: living as risen beings means living as beings who raise, "take the victims down from the cross," "give them new life." This is what Bishop Pedro Casaldáliga proclaims: "Because I shall be raised, I must go about raising and provoking resurrection. Only those who lose their life will save it. Every act of faith in resurrection has to have a corresponding act of justice, of service, of solidarity, of love."[7] Giving new life to the victims is fullness, and overcoming selfishness and the risks and fear it involves is triumph.

"The Firstborn within a Large Family": In Community with the Victims

The first generation of Christians thought that Jesus' resurrection had brought the universal resurrection close (1 Thess. 4:15, 17; 1 Cor. 15:51). This did not happen, but the intuition was kept: Jesus did not rise alone, but as "the firstborn within a large family" (cf. Rom. 8:29; 1 Cor. 15:3; Col. 1:18; Rev. 1:5). The resurrection implies communion of some with others, a logical presupposition in cultures in which individualism had not taken root: speaking of the "fullness" of an isolated individual makes little sense.

If the firstborn is someone who has been crucified, we can well understand the eschatological community as above all a community of the poor and victims—as is already implied in the tradition of the Maccabees—and then, by extension and analogously, as the universal community. Specifically, we can understand the Church as the Church of the poor. From Latin America comes the statement that the poor are "its principle of structuration, of organization, of mission."[8] And Moltmann, for his part, insists that the true Church is ultimately present in "the latent brotherhood of the universal judge hidden in the poor."[9] Christian life is "in community" and at its center is the firstborn, "a victim." The poor and the victims are not only the recipients of the Church's ethical activity; they are its center. They are the hinge that makes it operate in a Christian fashion.

"The Firstborn in Faith": Walking Humbly with God in History

Jesus is the firstborn in reaching God. But he is also the firstborn in journeying toward God. He walked in history doing justice and lovingkindness, as Micah says. He is the firstborn in faith (Heb. 12:2). I end with a consideration of "walking humbly with your God" (Micah 6:8).

I have already said how Jesus did this: he walked in trust in a God who is Father and in openness to a Father who is God. He walked resting in the Father and open to a God who did not let him rest. His resurrection was the ultimate encounter with this God-Father.

We are on the way toward this same God, as mysterious for us as he was for Jesus. And the fact that the end of this journey is presented to us as "resurrection" does not deprive the journey of mystery but heightens it. We can glimpse hope, but we have to go on walking.

I believe the experience of the ultimate mystery always happens through particular experiences. Through the elements of which they are composed, they make us think without the mind or heart relaxing; they attract without us being able to reach what is always further ahead of or further behind, or above, or below—us; they enlighten our sight without altogether dispersing the darkness; they gladden the heart without silencing Ivan Karamazov's protest.

This being so, I believe that both the reality called "resurrection" and the reality called God are made, so to speak, of suitable "material" for experiencing the mystery. "Resurrection" speaks of life and death, of the grace of some and the sin of others, the whole wrapped in finality—and without being able to "prove" anything. "God" offers himself to us as source of all life and as destiny that draws everything to greater fullness of life—in the midst of an infinite silence. Both realities are mystery.

It is true that props are always provided: for the resurrection—the testimonies of the New Testament, the timing of the accounts, the honesty of the witnesses;[10] for God—the philosophical proofs of God's existence, reflection down the ages, the testimonies that, in the end, it is more possible to become fully human than without God. But I think that in both cases there is a disproportion and that "the mystery remains a mystery." I do not believe that a concept of God eliminates or reduces what is mysterious in resurrection or that a concept of resurrection eliminates or reduces what is mysterious about God. What happens is that both converge, mutually reinforce each other, and lead to an ultimate mystery: God all in all.

Perhaps we can formulate it in Micah's words. If we walk in history intending to bring the crucified down from the cross, showing kindness to the despised and silenced victims, if we walk humbly and in the silence demanded by the memory of Ivan Karamazov, we can perhaps, inwardly, allow the ultimate mystery, God, to mold our life. And perhaps we can have the hope that at the end of our journey we may meet with this God in the community of the risen. There can be no mere "doctrine" to cover this. But we can make the experiment that hope is wiser than absurdity.

—*Translated by Paul Burns*

6

Helping Jesus' Legacy to Bear Fruit
in the Churches

Ellacuría on Archbishop Romero

During the twenty-fifth anniversary of Archbishop Romero's death, I have been recalling some of the incisive, luminous, encouraging words that Ignacio Ellacuría used to describe him. He described Monseñor as a great witness to Jesus, to his life and his destiny, his words and his work. So when I was asked to talk about Jesus in this Congress, I thought of doing it this way: presenting Jesus through Monseñor Romero—his witness—as Ellacuría saw Monseñor.

This may seem unnecessarily complex: from Ellacuría to Romero, and from Romero to Jesus. But it has an important advantage. The witnesses and martyrs best know Jesus, the witness and martyr, and make him present to us. What Ellacuría and Romero saw in Jesus, and especially the way Monseñor made him present among us, offer what we might call a "witness Christology," which obviously does not take the place of a "text Christology." But if the two are not somehow kept together, the text Christology can easily become excessively conceptual, without sufficient reality to put historical flesh on our thinking about Jesus Christ. It can degenerate, albeit subtly, into a "cheap Christology."[1]

It seems important to reflect on Jesus through Romero and Ellacuría, but it is even more important for Jesus, Archbishop Romero, and Ellacuría to shed light on and encourage us to find solutions to some of the present-day problems of the Church. I think these words of Pedro Casaldáliga say it well:

Published in *Revista Latinoamericana de Teología* 65 (2005): 117–37.

Out of the Christian faith itself comes a medicine chest of miracles and prosperities, a spiritual refuge in the face of evil and suffering, and a reserve of personal and communal co-responsibility in the transformation of society.[2]

Let us seek out this light and this spirit in the following points, which were fundamental in Monseñor's time but are not often considered today: the centrality of the *people*, who are so easily overlooked in the name of the people of God; the transcendence of God, which the Church must make present in Christian form as trans-descendence and condescendence; following Jesus as overcoming "docetism"—a perennial temptation of the Church—and the "unreality" that sometimes befall the faith; and the opening to grace, mercy, and holiness, which bear us up, and which may seem hidden or even displaced by the excessively worldly ways in which the Church carries out its mission.

Each of the following sections begins with a brief proposition, which is developed in two parts. In the first and longer part, we shall recall some of Ignacio Ellacuría's words about Archbishop Romero. In the second and shorter part, we shall recall some of Jesus' words on each respective theme.

The People

First proposition: The Church must keep the "people" and the "people of God" in mind, *seriously and together, so that it does not speak of the "people of God" apart from the people, nor of the "people" apart from the "people of God."*

"Hard to Speak of Archbishop Romero without Being Forced to Speak of the People"[3]

We begin with the theme of "the people," since it is not often thought about in the Church today. But apart from its intrinsic ecclesial and theological importance, it is useful and necessary to think about it, so that other more specifically Christian themes—like those discussed in the following sections: the transcendence of God, following Jesus, and grace—are infused with reality and not allowed to evaporate. This is how Ellacuría saw Monseñor's understanding of the people. We begin with this quote:

Mons. Romero's hope rested on two pillars. One was historical, his knowledge of the people, in whom he saw an ability to find a way out of the gravest difficulties. The other was transcendent, his conviction that ultimately God was a God of life and not of death, that the ultimate reality is good and not evil.[4]

We cannot express more clearly the importance Archbishop Romero placed on the people; along with God, they were a pillar of his hope. The centrality he gave "the people" is unusual today, so we need to be reminded of it. Like Archbishop Romero, Ellacuría knew the language that is usually used in the ecclesiastical world when it is necessary to refer to the people: "civil society," "citizens," or in the context of ecclesial reality, "lay" and "secular"—which suggests that the "people" of whom they speak are not the same as what the world calls "people": the human beings, immense majorities, organized or not, who live and suffer, saintly and sinful, poor people who do not take life for granted, whose deepest desire is to live. Before, in times of repression, it was said in addition that their most likely future would be either the slow death of poverty and hunger, of indignity and cultural death, or the violent death of repression.[5]

Monseñor loved those people—even before the "in addition"—not because they were holy and perfect, but with their limitations and sins, captive, oppressed, repressed, disparaged; he dedicated his human, Christian, and priestly life to their salvation. "Those who are in conflict with the people are in conflict with me. But my love is the people" (Homily of August 20, 1978).

Although he didn't explicitly talk about the "people," they were the reference point of many of the things he said in his homilies. That was certainly true of prophetic denunciation as a defense of the people: "I will not tire of denouncing abuse by arbitrary arrests, by disappearances, by torture" (Homily of July 24, 1979). And the prophecy focused on denunciation of unjust wealth: "Above all I denounce the absolutization of wealth. This is the great evil of El Salvador" (Homily of August 12, 1978). And of the lie: "We live in a world of lies, where no one believes in anything any longer" (Homily of March 18, 1979).

The people were also the reference point of the positive side of his message, of his hope: "The glory of the Lord will shine on these ruins" (Homily of January 7, 1979). And his faith: "The glory of God is the life of the poor."[6]

Ellacuría was deeply moved by the people as the essential reference point for Monseñor. He saw Archbishop Romero as truly and unconditionally incarnate in the people, an incarnation that meant in the first place giving the people all that he was and all that he had; and second, receiving from the people the best that they had. In any case Ellacuría

saw Romero accepting the same fate as the people, in the literal meaning of that word. "That incarnation earned him the love of the oppressed
people and the hatred of the oppressor. It earned him persecution, the
same persecution the people suffered. That is how he died and the reason he died."[7] And remember that he was referring to the people before
the "in addition."[8]

But Ellacuría was also moved by Monseñor's vision of the reality of
the people from the specificity of the Christian faith. Surprisingly, they
both saw the people in that same way, although I would not dare guess
who was theoretically and conceptually influencing whom. The fact is
that between 1977 and 1981 they both developed a theology of the
"people." The fundamental point of that theology was seeing the people
as a source of hope, as we have seen, and as bearer of salvation, about
which we shall say more; but it was especially important to analyze the
fact and the meaning of their suffering, in the light of faith. They described the people as the "crucified people" and as the "suffering servant of Yahweh."

On June 19, 1977, after the army left Aguilares having murdered
between one hundred and two hundred people, Archbishop Romero
went to celebrate the Eucharist and addressed these words to the terri-
fied peasants: "You are the Divine Pierced One"; that is, he identified
them literally with the crucified Christ. And in Holy Week 1978 he said
the same thing with great clarity: "We feel that the Christ of Holy Week,
with the cross on his back, is the people who are also bearing their
cross; we feel the crucified people in the Christ of the open and crucified
arms" (Homily of March 19, 1978). And in the homily of October 21,
1979, he identified the "people" with the "suffering servant of Yahweh."

Ellacuría did exactly the same. As a preparation for Puebla, in February 1978, he wrote a long essay comparing the suffering people to the
"suffering servant of Yahweh."[9] A few years later, exiled in Madrid in
1981, he affirmed in another famous article that "the sign of the times"
is always the historically crucified people.[10] In calling it a "sign of the
times," he meant it was "what characterizes an era" (cf. *Gaudium et
Spes* 4); it clearly was in those years a sign of the times, although Ellacuría
boldly added that it "always" is so. But we must remember what is
often forgotten: in Vatican II, "sign" also means "the presence of God
in history" (cf. *Gaudium et Spes* 11). Thus, for Ellacuría, the "crucified
people" stood for Christ crucified.

That was at the end of the 1970s, when as far as I can recall, no one
had ever spoken with such theological and christological depth about
the people. But let us go a step further. Both Ellacuría and Archbishop

Romero took the "people of God" seriously. The important thing, I think, is that they drew a connection between the two things and thus enhanced them both. "The people" lent historical, creaturely reality to the "people of God," and at the same time the "people of God" showed what the people were capable of giving: the mystery of God was invested in the people, critically of course, but clearly with a special preference.

Ellacuría gave a lot of thought to this. He did not back off on either side. His thesis was: there is no people of God without "the people," nor is there a people that cannot be people "of God." What I want to emphasize is that in drawing this connection he was deeply inspired by Monseñor. In a 1981 article[11] he described four characteristics of the true people of God, as he saw it in Archbishop Romero's thinking: "the preferential option for the poor," " historical incarnation in the people's struggles for justice and liberation," "adding Christian leaven to the struggle for justice," and "persecution for the sake of the reign of God in that struggle." Elements of both the "people" and the "people of God" were clearly present in this description. Thus he was speaking of a "people of God" intrinsically related to the "people."

There is food for thought in these words today, when we in the Church and society almost don't know what to do with the people in the struggle for justice and liberation. And we should not take it for granted. It was a miracle in that time. We should not be surprised that Ellacuría—the philosopher of historical reality, the theologian of liberation, the political analyst and mediator of great conflicts—should speak that way. But to speak in such radical language, with such radical concepts behind it, inspired by an archbishop, a man of the Church, precisely because he was a man of the Church, should be thought-provoking in our time. He saw in Archbishop Romero the historical ways in which the people were being shaped as people of God, and this gave credibility to what may have been Archbishop Romero's most specific contribution as a archbishop: adding Christian leaven to those historical struggles for justice and liberation. It is not easy to bring an historical struggle together with Christianity. Ellacuría saw that miracle taking place in Archbishop Romero's ministry.

We can also say that both Ellacuría and Archbishop Romero gave a name to the people, a name of dignity. They made reference to the "crucified people," the "Divine Pierced One," the "suffering servant of Yahweh." We emphasize this point, and treasure it, because our world not only distorts the reality of the peoples, especially in the affluent West, but also ignores and silences them as much as possible. In this situation, to call the people by name is no small thing. The greatness of

Archbishop Romero is that he called the people "divine" without diminishing their "human" reality, although of course he always sought to correct them, purify them, improve them. In any case he did not need to "baptize" the people from outside in order to commit himself totally to them. He did not in any way reflect the irony of Péguy: "They think they are in the eternal sphere because they are not in the temporal. Because they are not with man, they think they are with God"[12]—and we might add: "because they do not feel and suffer with the people, they think they are feeling and suffering with the people of God." We recall these words of Péguy as a powerful reminder not to fall into that common danger for Christians. Archbishop Romero was a classic example of how to avoid that danger.

We have left the most surprising part for the end. Both Ellacuría and Monseñor also saw salvation in that people. Remember that they both had hope in an "organized people," and they defended the need and legitimacy of popular organizations. They encouraged and corrected the organized people, and saw in them a potential for historical liberation. It is enough to remember that.[13] What we want to focus on now is the salvation that the people can bring, simply by being a suffering people as ours are.

Ellacuría said this clearly when he added the subtitle to his article, "The Crucified People: An Essay in Historical Soteriology." Archbishop Romero did not express the concept so systematically, and we should not stretch the meaning of his sometimes tortuous words on the subject. But I think he had the same insight, and expressed it in the language of traditional theology. I think his insight came from his sensitivity to the people and their suffering, and the fascination they held for him. Above all it came from his hope—his unfailing hope against hope—inspired by the great goodness of the people: "so much suffering, and so much goodness, cannot be in vain." It is that suffering people that cooperates, mysteriously, in liberation.

In the following homilies Monseñor draws on the traditional idea that suffering can bring redemption; yet this does not refer directly to redemption from sin, as traditional theology affirms, but to liberation from social injustice. Real poverty, he says tellingly, will save the world:

> God does not will this social injustice. . . . God demands justice, but he says to the poor, as Christ says to the oppressed who bear his cross: you will save the world if with your pain you give it not the conformism that is against God's will, but a restlessness for salvation . . . embodying whatever seeks to liberate the people in this situation. (Homily of December 24, 1979)

Blessed are those who hunger, blessed are those who weep, blessed are those who thirst for justice; . . . this is the poverty that will save the world. (Homily of September 11, 1977)

That the crucified people bring salvation is a theoretical concept, and needs to be historicized.[14] But it is important to uphold it, so as not to fall into another inherent temptation: thinking that salvation comes from above, either through miracles or worldly powers, or *only* through science, authority, hierarchy, and liturgy.

"He saw a great crowd; and he had compassion for them." (Mark 6:34)

Let us speak of Jesus now, without drawing facile parallels to what we have just said about Romero. There are not many Gospel texts to draw on, and the meaning of "people" has changed. There are similarities with Monseñor, for example in his prophetic denunciation of "oppression," though not in his support of popular "liberation" movements. But we can still say something important about Jesus' relationship with the people that can motivate the Church and the people to come together in our time, giving and receiving from one another.

In the Gospels, the people are the main reference point of Jesus' life. Without the people we cannot understand his everyday life. A great multitude from many places followed him (Mark 3:7). "They brought to him all who were sick or possessed with demons. And the whole city was gathered around the door" (Mark 1:32–33). And without the people we cannot understand his denunciation of the powerful, who "load people with burdens hard to bear" (Luke 11:46), and who "are called benefactors" while oppressing the people (Luke 22:25).

Like Monseñor, Jesus was deeply moved by the people's suffering. "He saw a great crowd; and he had compassion for them, because they were like sheep without a shepherd" (Mark 6:34). Matthew adds, "harassed and helpless" (Matt. 9:36). He gives hope to this people of the poor, and proclaims the good news of God's reign (Mark 1:14), so that in the oft-quoted words of J. Jeremias, "the kingdom belongs *only* to the poor."[15] And mysteriously he tells this crowd of hungry and thirsty people, sick and naked, foreigners and prisoners, that he (the Son of Man, the king) is one of them (Matt. 25:35–36). And in this one passage at least, he gives a proper name to Lazarus—the poor leper; symbol of the poor, oppressed, and humiliated people—but not to the rich man (Luke 16:20); this is no small thing in a world that does not give names to the poor. It does not mean that Jesus had a systematic idea of who the "people" were and what to do about them. But two things are clear, and from them we can draw fruitful and necessary impulses today.

The first is *the importance to Jesus of his relationship with what we have been calling the "people" without additional description.* He feels deep compassion for the people; he helps and embraces them, and he dies on the cross for defending them against their oppressors.[16] Beyond all doubt Jesus wanted the people to be what we now call the "people of God": that is the reason for his ethical demands, his insistence on fulfilling the commandments, especially the commandment of love, even love of the enemy, and on praying to the Father. And we recall what he proclaimed to everyone: it is in showing love to the suffering "people" that human life (Luke 10:29–37) and the life of salvation (Matt. 25:34–40) are judged.

It is essential for the Church to uphold Jesus' relationship with the people, with the suffering people. And it is not easy. History shows that very early on, with a few exceptions, Christianity shifted its gaze: "It did not look first at the creature's suffering, but at his guilt."[17] In the terms we are using here, it looked more directly at what makes it hard to be the "people of God" than at what permits living as the "people," created and loved by God. It became more interested in whether the people were the "people of God" than in the "people" themselves.

The second is *to ask ourselves whether Jesus expresses the soteriological, salvific dimension of the people.* Of course we need not look for it in the way Ellacuría thought, for example; here we are asking something more fundamental. Did Jesus not only see them as longing to be saved, but also as bringers of salvation, of salvific acts, which moved Jesus himself? With some audacity we may ask whether, in the words of Puebla (n. 1147), Jesus too was "evangelized by the poor"; we saw in an earlier chapter that he may well have been evangelized.

There is no need to fall into anachronisms. But these two things are fundamental: looking at the people as a people, suffering and hopeful, and letting ourselves be evangelized by them in some way, to some degree. These two things do not often happen in our time, and the Church would do well to return to them as Archbishop Romero did.

God

Second proposition: The Church must make transcendence present, but as trans-descendence and con-descendence. That is God's way.

"With Archbishop Romero, God Came through El Salvador."

In a mass he celebrated a few days after the assassination of Archbishop Romero, Ellacuría said, "With Archbishop Romero, God came through El Salvador." He saw that visit from God in Monseñor's whole life and destiny, his deeds and words. For now I shall focus only on Archbishop Romero's words, bearing in mind that his whole being appeared, or came near, in them. Obviously he did not mean that God came through El Salvador in Monseñor's words just because they were his. But many people experienced it that way, and I am personally convinced of it. It was Ellacuría's merit to have seen and expressed it.

Transcendence

Let us begin with some of Monseñor's most solemn words. Here God became present, we might say, as God—in his absolute transcendence. Here Romero speaks explicitly of God, without further description. This was sometimes the *God of total denunciation*, implacable, the God of "Cain, where is your brother?" (Gen. 4:9). Thus in the well-known last words of his last Sunday homily:

> Brothers, you belong to our own people, you are killing your own peasant brothers, and in the face of man's order to kill, the law of God should prevail: thou shalt not kill. No soldier is obliged to obey an order that is against the law of God. . . . So in the name of God, and in the name of this suffering people, whose cries go up to heaven more desperately every day, I ask you, I beg you, I order you in the name of God: Stop the repression! (Homily of March 23, 1980)

Other times it was the *blessing and humanizing God*, the irreplaceable "fountain of living water" (Jer. 2:13). In one of his last homilies, in the midst of the barbarism, he turned defenselessly and hopefully to that God:

> No one knows himself until he has met God. . . . I only wish that as the result of today's preaching, each of us would come to meet God. (Homily of February 10, 1980)

Ellacuría understood very well that Archbishop Romero was speaking of God, the unfathomable mystery, always beyond our grasp. And because God is like that, it is inherent in him to humanize history, to draw it to himself. This is how Ellacuría understood and expressed it:

Archbishop Romero never tired of repeating that political processes, no matter how pure and idealistic, are not enough to bring integral liberation to humanity. He understood perfectly what St. Augustine said: to be a man one must be "more" than a man. For him a merely human history, which only aspires to be human, will soon cease to be human. Neither humanity nor history is sufficient to itself. For that reason he always called us to transcendence. This theme was present in nearly all his homilies: God's word, God's action breaking down the limits of humanity. This transcendence never appeared as an abandonment of humanity, as a departure from human beings, but as an overcoming and a perfecting. A "there" that never abandoned the "here" but opened it up and pressed it forward.[18]

Trans-descendence and Con-descendence

Ellacuría, we might say, also saw this transcendent and infinitely other God come through in Monseñor's everyday words. This was a God whose steps are firm, self-lowering, and embracing; his transcendence became trans-descendence and con-descendence. It showed in much of what Monseñor said, even when he did not use the word "God." This God had the characteristics of the God of Jesus. Whenever Monseñor spoke— of anything important to human beings and the country—he communicated "something of God." He turned people toward God, and the people somehow knew, even if they could not fully explain it, that they had been turned toward God. Let us recall some of his words.

Monseñor spoke serious words in the midst of the social farce. "Robbery is in the air we breathe. And those who do not rob are called fools" (Homily of March 18, 1979). "They are playing with the peoples. . . . They are playing with human dignity . . ." (Homily of March 11, 1979). "We are living in a world of lies, where no one believes anything anymore" (Homily of March 18, 1979). Remaining serious in the face of reality, he described the dark side of the Church: "It would be a sad Church that only condemns, that only sees sins outside itself, without recognizing that it too is sinful" (Homily of July 8, 1979). And he recalled the obvious: "It is relatively easy to preach, but when we live what we preach . . . that is when the conflicts start" (Homily of July 16, 1978). By these words Monseñor meant: "We have to get serious. God is not like that. We can't play around with God." And *sub specie contrarii*, he aimed to discover God wherever human beings are acting honorably and seriously.

Honor and seriousness are among his best-known themes, in the midst of institutionalized concealment and lies, so we shall not repeat them here. Let us simply make two general observations. The first is that with incorruptible freedom, he also denounced those responsible for injustice, lies, and repression, whether it was the president of the republic, the Supreme Court of Justice, the Legislative Assembly, the armed forces, the security agencies, the oligarchy, or the U.S. government. In this way his denunciation was not only ethical, condemning evil deeds, but prophetic, condemning the perpetrators. Behind his words one could hear the God who denounces with absolute, incorruptible freedom: "Cain, Cain!"

The second observation is that his denunciation was, above all, merciful toward the victims. He denounced each and every act of barbarism, but he also, on principle, named the victims—"all" the victims—always giving some detail about the place and circumstances, even if that made his sermons long (two hours long in one case). This reflected not only or mainly the necessary meticulousness of juridical reports, but something deeper: the dignity of the victims. In this sense we can say that Monseñor was the initiator and guardian of "historical memory."

In the homily of October 30, 1977, in the part where he reviewed the events of the week, he explained the fivefold structure of his homilies, which expressed what was most important and closest to his heart: *comforting the victims, repudiating the crime, supporting the just demands of the people, giving hope to the people,* and *announcing the transcendence of God, beyond all our goals.* These were all the most important things, but the first among them was comfort, which came out of compassion and mercy. Behind these words one could hear the God of the exodus, of the prophets and Jesus, who "hears the cry of the suffering people," and who offers comfort and liberation.

Finally, they were words of humanity in the midst of inhumanity, always conveying flashes of God's humanity. With closeness to the people: "What a delight it is to see the people and the children gathering around one, coming up to one!" (Homily of August 12, 1979). With affection: "These are beloved names to me: Felipe de Jesús Chacón, 'Polín.' I have truly wept for them" (Homily of February 15, 1980). With respect for their dignity: "You are the Divine Pierced One" (Homily of July 19, 1977). With hope: "I am sure that so much blood spilled, so much sorrow, will not be in vain" (Homily of January 27, 1980). With humility: "I believe the bishop must always learn from the people" (Homily of September 9, 1979). And with credibility: "The pastor does not wish for security while it is not given to his flock" (Homily of July 2, 1979). And most human of all, with joy: "With these people it is not hard to be a good shepherd" (Homily of November 18, 1979). Behind these words one could hear the voice of the good God.

Today the powers of this world use many words that are perhaps more sophisticated and polished than in Monseñor's day. But God doesn't talk that way. And we need to say the same about everyday religious language: *God doesn't talk that way*. God talks the way Monseñor did. And because there is a relationship between word and presence, in Archbishop Romero's word God came through El Salvador. Not just any God, but the one who "remembers the littlest ones," as Gustavo Gutiérrez likes to say.

In any case Monseñor's word was always like "the word of God, clear and pure as the water coming down from the hills," as Rutilio Grande described it. That clarity and purity also made God present. Archbishop Romero said something similar during the time of barbarism: "God is not walking there, in puddles of blood and torture. God walks on clean paths of hope and love" (Homily of August 7, 1977). God was in Monseñor, and the people sensed it: "They had never felt God so near. . . . The people were opened up to Christian transcendence."[19]

"Jesus of Nazareth . . . went about doing good and healing all who were oppressed by the devil, for God was with him." (Acts 10:38)

We cannot develop this theme here, though it is central to the faith. I make only two points, based on what we have said, about God's walk with Monseñor.

The first is *how people understood God's presence in Jesus*. Soon after his crucifixion and resurrection, Jesus of Nazareth was recognized as the human being par excellence, the new Adam. But he was also recognized as the human being in whom God was made present, the "Son of God," the "word of God," "Lord," in God's place. The New Testament beautifully describes God's walk with Jesus: "For the grace of God has appeared . . . the goodness of God appeared" (Titus 2:11; 3:4). The reason is that if Jesus went about doing good, then "God was with him" (Acts 10:38). L. Boff expresses it magnificently: "Only God can be so human."

This is still important today. Obviously it is important to believers, but perhaps also for nonbelievers, however they express it, because it clearly means that reality is not absurd; in its depth there is goodness, salvation. What the Christian faith can contribute with simplicity and humility is that in Jesus, the transcendence of God becomes trans-descendence and con-descendence. As an important consequence, confessing that transcendence is not only a matter of doctrine and liturgy; it means making real the self-lowering (trans-descendence) and the embrace (con-descendence). That is how God came, in Jesus. The task and responsibility of the Church are obvious. Archbishop Romero's way of making God present, lowering himself and embracing others, is a great help.

The second point is that the faith not only confesses the fact of transcendence in a world that ignores or trivializes it; it affirms *the goodness of transcendence*. This is the "more" that attracts and forces reality to give "more" of itself. It is like a reserve of goodness, truth, and hope within history. That is said of Jesus Christ, and Archbishop Romero can help us understand it. "We feel the need for something transcendental, something that comes from outside" (Homily of January 7, 1979). Ellacuría affirmed the same thing, commenting on the homilies: "This transcendence never appeared as an abandonment of humanity, as a departure from human beings, but as an overcoming and a perfecting. A 'there' that never abandoned the 'here' but opened it up and pressed it forward."[20]

Today it is important—and urgent—to overcome what is dull and superficial, not to get trapped in the spirit of geometry but to move toward a spirit of finesse, as Pascal said. For that purpose it is helpful to think in terms of transcendence, and make it present in religious and secular terms. For the Church it is essential not only to mention it—"it is very easy to talk about transcendence," Monseñor used to say—but to make it present in real actions; to show that it is self-lowering, not pomp and triumphalism, and embrace, not authoritarianism and imposition.

Following

Third proposition: The Church is always in danger of promoting or tolerating an alienating faith, which leads to evasiveness (irresponsibility); and an infantilizing faith, which leads to unreality (the same old docetism). To overcome that danger, we must go back to following Jesus.

"Archbishop Romero was a model follower of Jesus of Nazareth."[21]

Ellacuría saw in Archbishop Romero a *pastor* who defended his people, a *prophet* who confronted the enemies of the people, and a *martyr*, faithful to the end to the God who sent him to save the people. But I also want to recall some sharper, less grandiloquent words that go to the heart of it all: "Monseñor was a model follower of Jesus of Nazareth."

What it was about Archbishop Romero that reminded him of Jesus is perhaps summed up in these words, spoken by Ellacuría about Jesus in a class: "Jesus had the justice to go to the depths, and at the same time he had the eyes and the bowels of mercy to understand human beings. . . . He was a great man." That doesn't explain all that Ellacuría saw in Jesus, but it says something that moved him deeply. And that is also what he saw as central in Archbishop Romero: *his enormous compassion in the face of the people's suffering, the justice to go to the root of things, and at the same time the hope—against hope—that he gave the people.*

Other things about Monseñor reminded him of Jesus, of course: his immense freedom in speaking the truth to everyone, with which he directly defended some and demanded radical conversion of others—he demanded it of the people too, but he demanded it most radically of their oppressors; and his firmness in the midst of persecutions, humiliations, and misunderstandings, even on the part of his fellow bishops. And Ellacuría was moved by his faith in the mystery of God the Father: Father, because Monseñor's rest was in him; and God, because the Father never let him rest.[22]

So Monseñor always reminded Ellacuría of Jesus of Nazareth. *He saw in Monseñor the same fundamental things that he saw in Jesus.* He not only saw someone who preached a particular kind of Jesus, but who made Jesus present. Archbishop Romero brought us to Jesus, but in a specific way: by following him, making him real in history, unconditionally. Archbishop Romero was a great believer, of course, but more importantly, we might say, he was a great follower.

Today this reminder seems very necessary. It is important for the Church to uphold specific things about Jesus in order not to invent—through its devotions and miraculous appearances—a Jesus who is very different from Jesus of Nazareth. But above all it must insist—and live the example—that we come to Jesus, most specifically, by following him. That is what Archbishop Romero did. He made the real life of Jesus real in his life, and thus made the Christianity he proclaimed something "real." Faith in Jesus was to be expressed in real things, which has never been and still is not obvious in our time.

Today's Churches are overflowing with triumphalism and enthusiasm, the search for success, as measured by large numbers and expressed by pomp and ostentation, sometimes to the point of apotheosis. All that takes us out of the reality of this humble creation. And they are over-flowing with infantilization: Christianity Lite, which provides apparent successes; an alienating credulity, confusing what Jesus called "being like children" (simple, trusting) with unthinking, uncritical childishness, which is not what Jesus meant. It takes us away from insecurity, but also away from the human condition. To put it in the form of a thesis, we think that kind of faith leads to unreality, as if God were taking care of history without us, by working miracles. That is ecclesial docetism. And it does not humanize.

To overcome the danger of unreality, we must return to what used to be called the "historical Jesus." What makes that return historical is "following." It is not a willful "going back" to the past, denying the possibility of new paradigms. It is returning to the irreplaceable nour-ishment of the beginning, to "that historical Jesus who so often fades away in hellenistic dogmatism and sentimental spiritualism, the poor Jesus, in solidarity with the poor, the Jesus crucified with the crucified ones of history."[23] Perhaps this will be clearer if we formulate it as a thesis.

Following Jesus makes us "be" like Jesus, which also means giving historical "flesh" to Jesus, "embodying" him in history. With all its limitations and even sins, following is what breaks down our separate-ness from Jesus. Followers of Jesus are those who in reality, not only by intention or in prayer, become like Jesus. They "are" like Jesus, some more and some less—and certainly this is what we have said about the martyrs of our Latin American peoples: they are "Jesuanic" martyrs, because they have lived like Jesus, they have loved the poor and de-fended them from their oppressors, they have denounced the oppres-sors' sins, they have persisted under the resulting persecution, and they have ended up on a cross like Jesus.[24] Following keeps faith from dis-solving out of its real substance.[25]

By being something real, following makes unconcealable the dialecti-cal, painful, and countercultural dimension of the Christian faith; this too, understandably, is easily ignored. Faith is "a victory" (1 John 5:4). And it is in the real process of following Jesus, not the mere intention, that we see what we have to struggle against and what battles we need to win: doubt, disillusionment, the temptation of carpe diem, persecu-tion, the understandable fear and the temptation to give up, Peter's "I don't know him," the costliness of "taking up your cross" that Jesus requires. So faith in Jesus is not only affirming truths about Jesus, how-ever sublime they may be, nor only practicing virtues, however legiti-mate and necessary they may be; it is rather a person's real and true commitment to the mystery of God, which waxes and wanes, becomes clearer and dimmer, as we follow Jesus. And it is a struggle against the *mysterium iniquitatis*, the idols and powers of the anti-kingdom. Then faith in Jesus is a victory, not only a peaceful affirmation of real or supposed truths, not even a blessed feeling of being embraced by divinity.

Let us also say that following is the epistemological beginning of the leap of faith. Following gives us the affinity we need to know who this Jesus is that we confess as Christ and Son of God. Apart from following we don't know exactly who we are talking about when we talk about Christ. Neither do we know what we are affirming when we say that we have faith; nor what we are denying when we say we do not have faith. The element of affinity is lacking. Faith becomes real in the real process of following, of struggling against real obstacles, that interfere with following. It is also in the process of following where the "most" specific part of faith can and does come in, the moment of transcendence. In following we experience history "giving more of itself," or "giving less of itself." It begins to "open," or to "close." Here we see the question of transcendence, more from the viewpoint of practical than purely theoretical reason: whether hope makes more sense than resignation, whether the greatest love—giving one's life—makes more sense than saving it. The answer may be yes, insofar as we clearly experience reality as infused with a higher mystery, of hope and love.

Monseñor clearly "was" like Jesus, reproduced his characteristics, and was his follower. We don't know whether he interpreted that following with exactly the same characteristics we have just described. But we do know some things, some of them very important. Following Jesus created great problems for Monseñor, and he ended up like Jesus. He recognized that himself. At his last spiritual retreat, a month before his death, he mentioned his two most serious problems to his confessor: the problems with his fellow bishops and his fear of death. So his following was, like faith, a "victory."[26] And the Church needs that in order to be a real Church.

"If any want to become my followers, let them deny themselves and take up their cross and follow me." (Mark 8:34)

Following Jesus is the specifically Christian problem of the Church, and it has been that way from the beginning. The first Christians soon recognized Jesus as "someone special." They did it in the Eucharist; they sang hymns in his honor and developed Christologies; they began to call him "Lord," "Son of God," "Head of creation"; and they hoped for his early return. But the wisest among them soon saw the danger of stopping there, and struggled against it. Paul did that, reminding the charismatics—we have called them enthusiasts, "unreal"—of Corinth that the wisdom of God is in the reality of a cross (1 Cor. 1:8–23), a scandal, and foolishness. They had forgotten Jesus, and some even denied him—as some Corinthians reportedly did, saying, "Let Jesus be cursed!" (1 Cor. 12:3)—because they thought they had found something better: an airy spirit.

Mark also saw the danger;[27] I want to say more about him, because he is one of the clearest examples of that serious warning against the enthusiastic, "lite," unreal understanding of Christianity. His Gospel was "troubling" to overly complacent Christians—and now I am thinking what Archbishop Romero's anniversary teaches us about how and how not to celebrate him.

The Gospel of Mark celebrates Jesus, but with great caution. It proclaims him "Son of God," yet it does not put that invocation in the mouth of the pious folk, but of demons (Mark 5:7) and a pagan, the Roman centurion (Mark 15:39). Moreover, this happens at the foot of the cross, before the ravaged body of that Son of God. He also calls Jesus "Messiah," but when that happens, Jesus himself says not to tell anyone.

Mark insists that faith in Jesus is neither triumphalistic, nor "lite," nor easy. It is serious, not at all obvious. It was not easy for his family, nor for his disciples—especially Peter—and certainly not for the theologians and priests of the time. And his Gospel ends abruptly, in Mark 16:8, almost leaving more questions than answers: the women "went out and fled from the tomb, for terror and amazement had seized them; and they said nothing to anyone, for they were afraid." That ending was so shocking that some verses were added later to soften the blow.

The Jesus who isn't interested in being called Messiah is interested in something different: "following." In the Gospels, "Follow me" is Jesus' first and last word to Peter, as Bonhoeffer reminds us.[28] In Mark, Jesus himself says it clearly: "If any want to become my followers, let them deny themselves and take up their cross and follow me" (Mark 8:34). Jesus calls us to follow, and there is no Christian life without responding, in substance, to that call; it takes priority over any other institutional requirement.

One last word from Mark about following. In the baptism scene the heavens open and Jesus hears the words of the heavenly Father (Mark 1:11). It is the call to his mission from on high, but historically, in fact, in his own way Jesus followed a path blazed by others. Mark tells it this way: "Now after John was arrested, Jesus came to Galilee, proclaiming the good news" (Mark 1:14; Matt. 4:12). Setting aside exegetical details for now, this means that Jesus began his own mission, relating it in some way to John's—and existentially, that seems to have been the case.

We know very well that there were similarities and differences between their specific missions,[29] but the point here is that Jesus was consciously pursuing, in a new and different way, what others had done before; Jesus himself thought of it in relation to the prophets of Israel. This awareness is also apparent in a very important moment of his life. The disciples went to tell him about the death of John, and "when Jesus heard this, he withdrew from there" (Matt. 14:13; Mark 6:30). He felt something like a premonition. The Jesus who called others to follow him also somehow found himself rooted in a tradition begun by others, in this case John, and before him the prophets of Israel. The stream he followed was not entirely new, although he shaped it in his own way.

It seems very important for the Church to remember this. In recent years the Salvadoran Church has passed through moments of Christian splendor. It has taken up the founding tradition of following Jesus and historicized that following into a stream. We can say that the stream was shaped this way: "When Rutilio Grande was murdered, Archbishop Romero began; when Archbishop Romero was murdered, Father Ellacuría began."[30] Rutilio, Monseñor, and Ellacuría, and many other men and women, historicized the fundamental Christian tradition and created a stream along which the tradition began to bear fruit. Each of them, in his or her own way, picked up the torch that the other had left. It was difficult and costly, but also joyful. They made something real out of the faith, Christianity, and the Church. That is what they have left to us.

Whatever may be the best historicization for today, whatever new paradigms have intervened, we cannot overlook this great fact about the Salvadoran Church. Like all Christian Churches, it must come back to the call of Jesus: "Follow me." But it has the privilege and responsibility of walking along the stream that the best people, their predecessors, left. And in any case it cannot fail to hear the call that comes from the poor, their powerful and demanding outcry. That kind of Church and faith will be a "real" Church and a "real" faith.

Grace

Fourth proposition. The Church needs "grace" in order to know what it must be and what it must do, and it needs "grace" to make them both real. Therefore it must set its eyes on Jesus.

"With this pastor it is so easy to be the people of God."[31]

To conclude the reflections in this article, let us say that Ellacuría saw a gift in Archbishop Romero, both in the newness and goodness that he brought to history, and in the power he gave others to carry it out. Ellacuría saw Monseñor as a grace for him and for the Salvadoran people, and it is very true that that Church and that people in the 1970s "deserved" a good shepherd.

That is how Ellacuría saw him. In 1985, when the UCA posthumously awarded Monseñor an honorary doctorate, Ellacuría said:

Certainly Archbishop Romero often asked for our collaboration, and this was a great honor for us, for the people he asked us to help, and for the cause he asked us to serve. . . . But in all this collaboration there was no doubt who was the master and who was the helper, who was the shepherd laying out the path and who was the assistant, who was the prophet unraveling the mystery and who was the follower, who was the motivator and who was motivated, who was the voice and who was the echo.[32]

The immediate context of these words was the accusation that the UCA had manipulated Monseñor—an issue that persists today in one form or another, as if God and the poor could not "manipulate" Archbishop Romero by themselves. With these words, Ellacuría wanted to clarify the truth and respond to the accusation. But he also wanted to make clear that Archbishop Romero was the leader, as he understood it: the one who steps forward and moves others by his example. He moved people to follow Jesus, which was not easy in those days, for it entailed risks, persecution, and martyrdom.

This was even clearer from what Ellacuría said next: "Along with what he used to say, 'with this people it is so easy to be a good shepherd,' we can say that 'with this shepherd it is so easy to be the people of God.' "[33] In this graphic way, Ellacuría was saying that Monseñor was a grace to the people. We were all graced.

Speaking personally, I think Monseñor was a grace to Ellacuría in a very special way. I often thought that Ellacuría might have considered himself, more or less, a colleague of Zubiri in philosophy and a colleague of Rahner in theology, his two most important teachers. But he never considered himself a colleague of Archbishop Romero, because he always saw Monseñor as going ahead of him. That was true of the way Archbishop Romero stood before the ultimate mystery, faith in God. As I have written, whatever may have been Ellacuría's faith, that faith was carried along—without diminishing the mystery of something so personal—by Archbishop Romero's faith.[34] In other words, he saw in Monseñor someone who had the power to "move him" in faith without imposing. That is grace.

"Looking to Jesus the pioneer and perfecter of our faith." (Heb. 12:2)

Jesus received, was "graced" by the faith he saw in the simple people; that is what made him, unashamedly, our brother (Heb. 2:11). But he is the greatest gift and grace: "grace and truth came through Jesus Christ" (John 1:17). Jesus is grace, the undeserved appearance of true humanity and divinity. But he is also grace because he gives us the power to be both human and divine.

That is what the letter to the Hebrews says. It shows us a community with problems, probably big ones: "You have not *yet* resisted to the point of shedding your blood" (Heb. 12:4). In this context the author gives them a long list of witnesses to the faith, ending with Jesus, "the pioneer and perfecter of our faith" (Heb. 12:2): Jesus is the "model" believer. But he also adds twice (Heb. 12:2, 3) that they should "look to Jesus," because from him comes the strength of faith, to live as they should live and to overcome the problems. "Consider him who endured such hostility against himself from sinners, so that you may not grow weary or lose heart" (Heb. 12:3). Jesus is also the believers' "strength." He goes ahead, moving us to follow him.

Let us end with what we said in the title of this chapter. We can no longer hide the fact of an "ecclesial winter" and a "turning back" from Medellín. We need to recover an evangelical Church, the Church of the poor. For that purpose we need to help Jesus' legacy to bear fruit. His spirit enlightens and encourages us. To help make Jesus present today we have offered the life, the faith, and the love of Archbishop Romero, seen rigorously and vigorously through the eyes of Ignacio Ellacuría.

—Translated by Margaret Wilde

Notes

1. The Crucified People and the Civilization of Poverty

[1]Two theses on this subject are worth mentioning: M. Maier, *Theologie des Gekreuzigten Volkes: Der Entwurf einer Theologie der Befreiung von Ignacio Ellacuría und Jon Sobrino* (doctoral thesis, University of Innsbruck, 1992); and K. Burke, *The Ground beneath the Cross: Historical Reality and Salvation in the Theology of Ignacio Ellacuría* (Washington, DC: Georgetown University Press, 2000).

[2]"Hacia una fundamentación filosófica del método teológico latinoamericano," *Estudios Centroamericanos* 322–23 (1975): 419.

[3]"La teología como momento ideológico de la praxis eclesial," *Estudios Eclesiásticos* 207 (1978): 457.

[4]"Aporte de la teología de la liberación a las religiones abrahámicas en la superación del individualismo y del positivismo," *Revista Latinoamericana de Teología* 10 (1987): 9.

[5]"Teología en un mundo sufriente: La teología de la liberación como *intellectus amoris*," *Revista Latinoamericana de Teología* 15 (1988): 243–66.

[6]"Hacia una fundamentación," 419.

[7]Ibid. This suggests, in other words, that reality does not just suddenly "appear" in things. Rahner said that "reality wants to have a word," but we have to let it speak, and once it has spoken we must respect its word. The apostle Paul warns that this is not self-evident; he sees in human beings the possibility—and the fact—of wickedly suppressing the truth (Rom. 1:18).

[8]*El pueblo crucificado: Ensayo de soteriología histórica* (Mexico: CRT, 1978), reproduced after his assassination in *Revista Latinoamericana de Teología* 18 (1989): 305–33.

[9]"Discernir el 'signo' de los tiempos," *Diakonía* 17 (1981): 58.

[10]"Función liberadora de la filosofía," *Estudios Centroamericanos* 435–36 (1985): 50.

[11]This example may seem oversimplistic. Citizens of the United States "exist," "they are", that is clear because, among other things, they have their own "calendar." On this calendar, 9/11—or in Spain, 3/11—really exists. But 10/7 (2001) and 3/30 (2003), when the Western nations bombed Afghanistan and Iraq, do not exist. The Third World does not have a "calendar"; it does not exist.

[12]The bishops added another, equally important sign: "a longing for total emancipation from all slavery, for personal growth and collective integration" (*Introduction* 4).

[13]"El pueblo crucificado," 326.

[14]"Quinto Centenario de América Latina: ¿Descubrimiento o encubrimiento?" *Revista Latinoamericana de Teología* 21 (1990): 281ff.

[15]"El desafío de las mayorías pobres," *Estudios Centroamericanos* 493–94 (1989): 1078.

[16]Quoted in Ellacuría, "El pueblo crucificado," 308.

[17]*The Prayer of Saint Francis* (Maryknoll, NY: Orbis Books, 2001), 81.

[18]As I write this, I am reading the following headlines from the BBC Web site: "In the world a child dies of hunger every five seconds"; "842 million people are hungry";

"The Millennium Goals will not be met"; "Increasing gap between poor and rich."

[19]"Lectura latinoamericana de los *Ejercicios Espirituales* de san Ignacio," *Revista Latinoamericana de Teología* 23 (1991): 119–24. More specifically, "Las iglesias latinoamericanas interpelan a la Iglesia de España," *Sal Terrae* 3 (1982): 230. With regard to the historical forms of this praxis, Ellacuría recommended a series of tasks— knowledge to develop models facilitating the life of the majorities, promotion of popular organization, negotiation to bring an end to the war—and he worked to bring the Church and the society into these activities. To this I only want to add what I have already hinted at. By giving the victims names, bringing them out of anonymity, he acknowledges their existence; think of the nonexistence to which sub-Saharan Africa and Afghanistan have been relegated. And he acknowledges their "dignity" by proclaiming, in Christian language, that today they are the "crucified Christ," the "suffering servant of Yahweh."

[20]Enrique Gómez García, a Zubiri scholar, finds in his thought a certain philosophical basis for the idea of the *graciousness* of reality. Gómez says: "the 'graciousness' contained in reality, which only people with spirit are able to perceive as the provident presence of God in creation, is more explicitly developed in the Zubirian understanding of the power of the real, which promotes the dimension of fundamentality." "De la 'espiritualidad de lo real' a la 'filosofía de la realidad': Aportes de X. Zubiri a la espiritualidad de la liberación," *Revista de Espiritualidad* 63 (2004): 548–49.

[21]"La UCA ante el doctorado concedido a monseñor Romero," *Estudios Centroamericanos* (1985): 168.

[22]Some reflections in this section appeared in "Epílogo: Revertir la historia," *Concilium* 308 (2004): 145–54.

[23]"El desafío," 1078.

[24]"El reino de Dios y el paro en el Tercer Mundo," *Concilium* 180 (1982): 588–96; "Misión actual de la Compañía de Jesús," written in 1983 and published posthumously in *Revista Latinoamericana de Teología* 29 (1993): 115–26; "Utopía y profetismo," *Revista Latinoamericana de Teología* 17 (1989), also published in I. Ellacuría and J. Sobrino, eds., *Mysterium Liberationis: Conceptos fundamentales de la teología de la liberación I* (Madrid: 1994), 393–442, and (San Salvador: 1991), 393–442; "Utopia and Prophecy in Latin America," *Mysterium Liberationis: Fundamental Concepts of Liberation Theology* (Maryknoll, NY: Orbis Books, 1993), 289–327.

[25]"Utopía," 170.

[26]Ibid.

[27]Ibid., 173.

[28]An interesting fact: I do not know whether and how much things have changed, but only ten years ago the U.S. economy consumed a third of the annual global production of mineral resources, in order to maintain the accustomed consumption level of 6 percent of the world population. See I. Zubero, *Las nuevas condiciones de la solidaridad* (Bilbao: 1994), 92.

[29]"Quinto Centenario," 277.

[30]Ibid., 282.

[31]"Utopía," 173.

[32]Ibid., 152.

[33]I. Ellacuría, "La Iglesia de los pobres, sacramento histórico de liberación," *Estudios Centroamericanos* (1977): 717.

[34]"Historización de los derechos humanos desde los pueblos oprimidos y las mayorías populares," *Estudios Centroamericanos* 502 (1990): 590. See also what I wrote in "Los derechos humanos y los pueblos oprimidos. Reflexiones histórico-teológicas," *Revista Latinoamericana de Teología* 43 (1998): 79–102.

[35]"Historización de los derechos humanos," 590.

[36]Ibid.

[37]Ibid., 591.

[38]Ibid., 593.
[39]Ibid., 590.
[40]Ibid., 593.
[41]Ibid.
[42]In *Revista Latinoamericana de Teología* 54 (2001): 235–53.
[43]"A los quinientos años: 'descolonizar' y 'desevangelizar,'" *Revista Latinoamericana de Teología* 16 (1989): 118. Casaldáliga later spoke of the civilization of "solidary poverty."
[44]"Utopía," 170.
[45]"El reino de Dios," 595.
[46]"Utopía," 170.
[47]Interview in *Éxodo* 78–79 (2005): 66.
[48]"Utopía," 172.
[49]"El desafío," 1078.
[50]"Utopía," 172.
[51]"Misión actual," 119–20.
[52]"La UCA ante el doctorado concedido a monseñor Romero," 168.
[53]*Terremoto, terrorismo, barbarie y utopía: El Salvador, Nueva York, Afganistán* (Madrid, 2002), 125-135; (San Salvador, 2003), 129–40; *Where Is God? Earthquake, Terrorism, Barbarity, and Hope* (Maryknoll, NY: Orbis Books, 2004), 71–105.
[54]He wrote an important article about this: "El papel de las organizaciones populares en la actual situación del país," *Estudios Centroamericanos* 372–73 (1979).
[55]"Utopía," 141.

2. Depth and Urgency of the Option for the Poor

[1]See X. Alegre, "Un silencio elocuente o la paradoja del final de Marcos: 'Y no dijeron nada a nadie porque tenían miedo' (Mc 16, 8b) II," *Revista Latinoamericana de Teología* 53 (2003): 149–55.
[2]Something similar happens in the book of Amos. Its original ending is very sharp: "All the sinners of my people shall die by the sword" (9:10); another, hopeful ending (vv. 11–15) was added later. The hope expressed in these verses is also a central theme in the Old Testament, but the need to add them shows how difficult it was to maintain the sharpness of Amos's words.
[3]Ignacio Ellacuría usually talked about the poor in their different dimensions: social (socioeconomic, dialectical, political, ethical-political, and ethical-personal), theologal, christological, soteriological, and ecclesiological; see "Pobres," in *Conceptos fundamentales de pastoral* (Madrid, 1987), 786-802. In this way he showed *in actu* their depth and mystery.
[4]*La Iglesia en la fuerza del Espíritu* (Salamanca, 1978), 26 (English translation: *The Church in the Power of the Spirit* [New York: Harper & Row, 1977]).
[5]In existential reality we are standing in the hermeneutical circle. We affirm that the poor bring us to God and Christ; but once we know that God and that Christ, they show us that their place is among the poor, which is what the revealed word shows.
[6]Let us briefly say that the messianic praxis of Jesus was also historically shaped in relationship with the poor, as regarding both the content of his activity (the needs, hopes, and limitations of the poor) and his personal attitudes (proclamation and denunciations, joys, risks, endurance to the end). We cannot mechanically deduce the messianic praxis of Jesus from the poor of his time, but neither can we understand his praxis without making that situation a central consideration. See R. Aguirre, *Ensayo sobre los orígenes del cristianismo: De la religión política de Jesús a la religión doméstica de Pablo* (Estella, 2001), 24–38.

[7]Words of Cardinal Giacomo Lercaro in the first session of the Second Vatican Council, December 6, 1962. An almost complete version of the text can be seen in T. Cabestrero, "En Medellín la semilla del Vaticano II dio el ciento por uno," *Revista Latinoamericana de Teología* 46 (1999): 65–67.

[8]A. Pieris, "Cristo más allá del dogma: Hacer cristología en el contexto de las religiones de los pobres," *Revista Latinoamericana de Teología* 52 (2001): 14.

[9]Miguel Lamet reports that he interviewed Fr. Pedro Arrupe about important aspects of his life as general of the Society of Jesus. Fr. Arrupe spoke with difficulty and effort, but also very freely, because he was lying in an infirmary bed. When Lamet asked about Medellín, he said: "Medellín did a lot of good. It was stronger and more prophetic than Puebla. Many positive things were achieved as a result of Medellín" (N. Alcover, ed., *Pedro Arrupe: Memoria siempre viva* [Bilbao, 2001], 237).

[10]"Situación y tareas de la teología de la liberación," *Revista Latinoamericana de Teología* 50 (2000): 111.

[11]Ibid., 109.

[12]Ibid.

[13]"Iglesia y solidaridad con los pobres en Africa: Empobrecimiento antropológico," in *Identidad, africana y cristiana* (Estella, 1999), 283. Mveng was the first Camerounian Jesuit. He was assassinated in 1995.

[14]"Above all we must avoid letting the necessary and urgent attention to the suffering and hopes of the poor lead to useless theological infighting. This would cause situations of exclusiveness and mistrust, which weaken the daily struggle of the dispossessed for justice and for respect of their cultural and religious values—because these are convergent and complementary perspectives. Also for their right to be equal and, at the same time, different" ("Situación y tareas," 112).

[15]Much of the following section is further developed in "La utopía de los pobres y el reino de Dios," *Revista Latinoamericana de Teología* 56 (2002): 145–70.

[16]"La compasión: Un programa universal del cristianismo en la época del pluralismo cultural y religioso," *Revista Latinoamericana de Teología* 55 (2001): 27.

[17]Ibid., 28.

[18]Homily of July 29, 1979.

[19]In this context I want to recall Ellacuría's four requirements for effective thinking and praxis: *objectivity* to know things as realities; *realism* to take the steps that reality demands and permits; *prophecy* to unmask and absolutely condemn the evils and, especially, their causes; and *utopia* to show the way—without debate—and give energy to follow it.

[20]A ninety-meter wall monument was recently inaugurated in San Salvador with the names of 24,965 civilians disappeared or murdered between 1970 and 1991, although over half the people named are still missing. The initiative and construction of the monument came from civil society organizations, not the government, although the United Nations Truth Commission gave the government that responsibility in 1993.

[21]*In IV Sent.*, dist. XLIX, q. V, a.3, q.2, ad 11.

[22]It is important today to continue sharpening the concept of martyrdom so as not to reduce it to the fate of witnesses or militants, whether Christian or not, and so that these majorities will be included in their own right. See T. Okure, J. Sobrino, F. Wilfred, eds., "Repensar el martirio," *Concilium* 299 (2003): monographic issue.

[23]"Hacia el futuro: ética, política y derechos humanos," *Revista Latinoamericana de Teología* 58 (2003): 50.

[24]Ibid. See also I. Ellacuría, "Historización de los derechos humanos desde los pueblos oprimidos y las mayorías populares," *Estudios Centroamericanos* 502 (1990): 589–96; and J. Sobrino, "Los derechos humanos y los pueblos oprimidos. Reflexiones histórico-teológicas," *Revista Latinoamericana de Teología* 43 (1998): 79–102.

[25]J. Comblin, quoted in ibid.

[26]Homily of July 15, 1979.

[27]Homily of June 24, 1979.

[28]See J. Sobrino, "Los mártires latinoamericanos: Interpelación y gracia para la Iglesia," *Revista Latinoamericana de Teología* 48 (1999): 307–30; "Los mártires: interpelación para la Iglesia," *Concilium* 299 (2003): 159–69. See also *Witnesses to the Kingdom: The Martyrs of El Salvador and the Crucified Peoples* (Maryknoll, NY: Orbis Books, 2003).

[29]"Las iglesias latinoamericanas," 230.

[30]"La autoridad doctrinal del pueblo de Dios," *Concilium* 200 (1985): 71–81. Aloysius Pieris also mentions the "magisterium of the poor" as one of the three central elements in an Asian, non-Euroamerican theology, in *Liberación, inculturación, diálogo religioso* (Estella, 2001), 257.

[31]J. B. Metz, in "La compasión," 30, 31.

3. *Extra Pauperes Nulla Salus*

[1]"El desafío de las mayorías pobres," *Estudios Centroamericanos* 493–94 (1989): 1078.

[2]"Utopía y profetismo," *Revista Latinoamericana de Teología* 17 (1989): 170ff.

[3]Ibid.

[4]Ibid.

[5]Cf. "El desafío," 1076ff.

[6]Ibid., 1078.

[7]Ibid.

[8]*Veo a Satán caer como el relámpago* (Barcelona, 2002), 209 (English translation: *I See Satan Fall Like Lightning* [Maryknoll, NY: Orbis Books, 2001]).

[9]Ibid.

[10]Ibid., 210.

[11]Ibid., 209.

[12]"Utopía necesaria como el pan de cada día," a public letter January 2006.

[13]"It receives death threats from big international finance capital, which seeks to make the invisible hand of the market the sole, supreme authority of history" (J. Ziegler, special reporter of the United Nations for the right to food, in "Entrevista," *El País*, May 9, 2005).

[14]"Utopía necessaria," op. cit. In the Old Testament, the holocaust (*shoah* in Hebrew, *holocaustos* in Greek) is not a metaphor taken from the cultic sacrifices, in which the victim was totally destroyed. To designate these, the Pentateuch uses the terms *korban* and *'olah. Shoah* is used, after the exile, to describe the *historical* destruction and extermination of human beings. Luis Sebastián has just published the book, *África, pecado de Europa* (Trotta, 2006); he has recourse to religious language, the language of sin, since no other civilized, democratic language appears to have the force that is needed to speak of Africa properly.

[15]Ibid.

[16]F. Mayor Zaragoza, "Tener presente el futuro," *El País*, June 6, 2006, 15.

[17]Report of Amnesty International, 2005.

[18]"To help Africa you have to understand it first. We don't want you to think for us." From an interview in Bamako, capital of Mali, during the celebration of the World Social Forum, January 19–23, 2006. The author was born in Mali fifty-eight years ago. She has a doctorate in social psychology and psychopathology, and is former minister of culture, consultant for the United Nations, community leader, and writer.

[19]See T. Forcades i Vila, *Los crímenes de las grandes compañías farmacéuticas* (Barcelona, 2006).

[20]L. de Sebastián, *Problemas de la globalización* (Barcelona, 2005), 4.

[21]"Very few people are left today who say that poverty is the result of injustice" (J.

Vitoria, "Una teología de ojos abiertos. Teología y justicia. Perspectivas," *Revista Latinoamericana de Teología* 69 [2006]). And even fewer relate it to capitalism.

[22]Taking up again "the silences of the Church's social doctrine," an idea recently reiterated by Yves Calvez, José Comblin states that said doctrine "does not question the system." It criticizes the adjectives, such as *savage* capitalism, but not capitalism as such. John Paul II's encyclical *Laborem Exercens* did treat the question; he stated that labor was the fundamental principle of economics and anthropology (see the commentary of I. Ellacuría, "Conflicto entre trabajo y capital en la presente fase histórica. Un análisis de la Encíclica de Juan Pablo II sobre el trabajo humano," *Estudios Centroamericanos* 409 [1982], 1008-24). This insight of the Pope did not stand out in the Church's public discourse, probably because of its resemblance to the thought of Marx, especially during the 1980s, when Reagan was determined to crush the revolutionary movements in Nicaragua, El Salvador, and Guatemala. Politically, any direct questioning of capitalism was considered to be going too far. In this way, the Church's social doctrine was co-opted. Ellacuría had already stated that, whereas the Church's social doctrine aimed more at (merely) moderating capitalism, liberation theology aimed more at humanizing socialism.

[23]*La oración de San Francisco* (Santander, 1999), 98.

[24]"¿Quién manda en el mundo?" *Servicios Koinonía*, January 20, 2006.

[25]We have offered enough quotes so to make the point by sheer accumulation, and I ask pardon that I am not always able to give references to the precise sources from which they are taken.

[26]"In our time it can be estimated that some 30% of humanity lives in dire poverty, which is much less than in earlier epochs, when the figure might have reached 80 or 90% of the total. But it is also true that the kings, nobles, bankers, and landlords of the past were economic pigmies compared to the rich people of today. Modern societies are becoming ever more dual societies (two societies in one), composed of two parts that live separately and far apart, with very different standards of living and very different ways of using the material goods and the culture produced in the societies. . . . The wealth/poverty duality is presently more extreme than it has ever been before in history. . . . The inequality would not be so grievous if those who are worst off were doing okay. The awful thing is that those who are worst off are not doing well at all" (L. de Sebastián, *Problemas de la globalización*, 2–4).

[27]L. Boff comments: "I am frankly alarmed at the catastrophe that will follow on the entrance of this giant into the capitalist circuit, which is characterized not only by exploitation of people, but also by destruction of the environment."

[28]Some 80 percent of Chinese businesses, according to deputies of the Chinese Communist Party, do not offer their workers contracts. And in the 20 percent that do, the contract is for less than one year. The "Chinese economic miracle" is producing serious evils: corruption and a huge and growing income gap. It should be added that Chinese development has implied underdevelopment in other countries, especially in the Third World. Something similar could occur with India.

[29]Allow me to use the following words of K. Rahner, written in a completely different context. In the sixties, in the face of the lamentable situation of the dogmatic theology being used, in his first great article on the Trinity, he wrote criticizing the very way the doctrine was approached: the method "is shown to be false simply by observing its effective reality: *it just can't be that way*" ("Warnings about the Dogmatic Treatise 'De Trinitate,'" in *Escritos de Teología* IV [Madrid, 1962], 117). John XXIII wanted to communicate something similar before the council, when he asked that "the windows of the Church be thrown open." Inside the church, you could not breathe pure air.

[30]Read again the magnificent book of Albert Nolan, *God in South Africa* (Grand Rapids: William B. Eerdmans, 1988).

[31]Many years ago H. Marcuse was saying this in *One-Dimensional Man*.

[32]I. Ellacuría, "Discernir 'el signo' de los tiempos," *Diakonía* 17 (1981): 58.

[33]The critique of democracy is an important long-range task. Suffice it to say now that Ellacuría was not satisfied with judging only its procedural dimension. Democracy has to be understood essentially as a form of government that seeks the common good, the necessary basis for establishing a society that is inclusive, just, and in solidarity with the least well off. Democracy presents a problem not only in its political dimension, but also—and equally importantly—in its social and economic dimensions. Briefly, a social democracy is one that makes it possible to change the unjust conditions in which the majority of people live. Accordingly, Ellacuría thought that democracy has meaning only insofar as it is based on the reality of the poor majorities, those large impoverished sectors that are excluded by the dominant groups. This is what must be verified. If the verification is not positive, there is not much sense in talking of democracy.

[34]We offer some examples. "Official development aid is at its lowest level in the last fifty years," according to Kofi Annan (1999). "Western aid to the Third World has done nothing but decrease, and I believe that is a crime," said James Wolfenson, former president of the World Bank (2000). Flavio Miragaya Perri, Brazil's ambassador to the FAO, speaks of an original sin, committed by the colonial powers from time immemorial. And he adds: "First World aid to combat hunger and poverty (around 50 billion dollars annually) is equal to one-seventh of the subsidies that are given to their farmers (350 billion dollars) in order to grow cheaper products that have a competitive advantage in the market" (taken from *Co-Latino*, San Salvador, June 1, 2004).

[35]Such is the text that was read at the demonstration against poverty in Madrid on October 21, 2006.

[36]Ibid.

[37]Ziegler, op. cit. Irene Khan, director of Amnesty International, says that "governments are losing their moral compass" (September 11, 2001).

[38]Similarly, we should not trivialize the feast of the "holy innocents" or reduce it to a decorative Christmas motif in our liturgy. Whatever the historical reality of the story, it speaks of innocent children who were murdered cruelly.

[39]Remember that for Plato the sphere is the symbol of perfection (*Symposium* XIV–XV, 189c–192d).

[40]The Cristianisme i Justicia Foundation published a pamphlet with the title "¿Mundialización o conquista?" (Barcelona, 1999).

[41]"Progreso y precipicio: Recuerdos del futuro del mundo moderno," *Revista Latinoamericana de Teología* 54 (2001): 302 (emphasis mine).

[42]L. de Sebastián, "Europa: globalización y pobreza," *Concilium* 293 (2001): 743. More recently he wrote: "I understand globalization as the result, still partial and undetermined, of a process that tends to unify the national markets of goods and services . . . within great world markets, at the same time that the logic of the market (privatization) is introduced into the spheres and activities of humanity's social life" (*Problemas de la globalización*, 28).

[43]"Problemas," Ibid., 4.

[44]"Europa," 743.

[45]In *Carta a las Iglesias* 544 (2005): 11.

[46]Taken from *Zenit*, January 23, 2006.

[47]Words of González Calvo, director of the magazine *Mundo Negro*.

[48]John Paul II, *Pastores Gregis*, October 16, 2003, no. 67 (emphasis mine).

[49]F. Mayor Zaragoza, op. cit.

[50]H. Pinter, *Discurso de aceptación del Premio Nobel de Literatura*, December 7, 2005.

[51]J. Taubes, interview published in *Messianesimo e cultura: Saggi di politica, teologia e storia* (Milan, 2001), 399–400.

[52]"El desafío," 1080.

[53]The formula is present, in a way, in Marx: salvation comes from a social class at the

bottom of history. Such is the thought of I. Ellacuría ("El pueblo crucificado," in *Conversión de la Iglesia al reino de Dios* [San Salvador, 1986], 29–31), although we should recall that Marxism does not see salvific potential in the *lumpenproletariat*. To my understanding, the social philosophy that is the basis of democracy does not address the issue either. At the most, it would make poor people citizens with the same rights as others, but it does not place them, either in theory or in practice, at the center of society, nor does it make them, precisely as poor people, the specific bearers of salvation. Neither does the Church do so, either in theory or in practice.

[54]Przywara insists on this. Reality is always greater than our ideas. The bigger reality is, the more deferential our ideas should be. The *via negativa* need not be, then, an expression of lack of knowledge about reality, but may well be an expression of respect and humility in the face of reality—and of a more profound knowledge.

[55]Interview in *Éxodo* 78–79 (2005): 66.

[56]"El poder, ¿para qué?, ¿para quiénes?" *Páginas* 194 (2005): 50–61.

[57]"Golpeando suavemente los recursos locales de la esperanza," *Concilium* 308 (2004): 104.

[58]"Las bienaventuranzas, carta fundacional de la Iglesia de los pobres," in *Conversión de la Iglesia al reino de Dios* (San Salvador, 1985), 129–51.

[59]"Misión actual de la Compañía de Jesús," *Revista Latinoamericana de Teología* 29 (1993): 119ff.

[60]"Cristo más allá del dogma. Hacer cristología en el contexto de las religiones de los pobres" (I), *Revista Latinoamericana de Teología* 52 (2001): 16.

[61]"Iglesia y solidaridad con los pobres de África," in *Identidad africana y cristiana* (Estella, 1999), 273ff.

[62]He dedicated much thought to this in his final years. See "Misión actual de la Compañía de Jesús," 115–26 [the text was written in 1981]; "El reino de Dios y el paro en el Tercer Mundo," *Concilium* 180 (1982): 588–96; "Utopía y profetismo desde América Latina: Un ensayo concreto de soteriología histórica," *Revista Latinoamericana de Teología* 17 (1989): 141–84.

[63]"La misión en la Iglesia latinoamericana actual," *Revista Latinoamericana de Teología* 68 (2006): 191. In addition to this, the author insists that the poor are the ones to whom the mission is principally aimed.

[64]"Lectura latinoamericana de los *Ejercicios espirituales* de san Ignacio," *Revista Latinoamericana de Teología* 23 (1991): 132.

[65]See what we wrote in *Jesucristo liberador. Lectura histórico-teológica de Jesús de Nazaret* (San Salvador, 1991), 220–23 (Madrid, ⁴2001) (English translation: *Jesus the Liberator: A Historical-Theological View* [Maryknoll, NY: Orbis Books, 1992]). In turn, we were inspired by I. Ellacuría, "Pobres," in *Conceptos fundamentales de pastoral* (Madrid, 1983), 786–802.

[66]Puebla mentions this in no. 1142, in speaking of God's option for the poor and the reasons for it, but we believe it is equally valid for describing the potential of poor people to move to conversion.

[67]Adorno says that "it is necessary to set up perspectives in which the world appears disturbed, alienated, showing its cracks and tears, beggarly and deformed" (*Minima Moralia* [Madrid, 1987], 250).

[68]Bonhoeffer says that in the presence of Lazarus a miracle can occur: "what the rich man has not seen, that his world is a world of death," quoted in M. Zechmeister, "Grito y canto," *Revista Latinoamericana de Teología* 69 (2006).

[69]"El desafío," 1076.

[70]P. Casaldáliga, "Del desencanto inmediatista a la utopía esperanzada," *Concilium* 311 (2005): 156.

[71]"Quinto centenario de América Latina: ¿Descubrimiento o encubrimiento?" *Revista Latinoamericana de Teología* 21 (1990): 282.

[72]To these three reflections of Ellacurían origin we are accustomed to add a fourth: "letting reality bear with us." That happens in the world of the poor.

[73]"Pobres," 796. Recall also that Puebla (no. 1137) speaks of the effectively political value of the poor: "they have begun to organize in order to live their faith integrally, and therefore also in order to claim their rights." And it comments: "Faith thus makes them a political force for liberation."

[74]We have analyzed this in greater detail in "Bearing with One Another in Faith: A Theological Analysis of Christian Solidarity," in *The Principle of Mercy* (Maryknoll, NY: Orbis Books, 1994), 144–72.

[75]"Palabras en el doctorado *Honoris Causa* en Ciencia políticas al presidente de Costa Rica Dr. Óscar Arias," mimeographed text.

[76]See what I wrote in *Jesus the Liberator*, 219–32.

[77]C. Díaz, *Monseñor Óscar Romero* (Madrid, 1999), 95–96.

[78]In "Teología cristiana después de Auschwitz," *Concilium* 195 (1984): 214ff. Today the victims of Auschwitz are still remembered, and they are recalled also in order to find in them salvation. Thus do we recall D. Bonhoeffer, E. Stein, E. Hillesum. . . .

[79]Taken from J. Vitoria, "Una teología de ojos abiertos."

[80]Quote from a nun who has spent many years in the Great Lakes region.

[81]A more detailed account can be found in "América Latina: lugar de pecado, lugar de perdón," *Concilium* 204 (1986): 226.

[82]See what we wrote in "Jesuanic Martyrs in the Third World," in *Witnesses to the Kingdom: The Martyrs of El Salvador and the Crucified Peoples* (Maryknoll, NY: Orbis Books, 2003), 119–32.

[83]As regards the salvation the martyrs offer to the Church, see my essay, "The Latin American Martyrs: Challenge and Grace for the Church," in *Witnesses to the Kingdom*, 134–54.

[84]Important is Moltmann's criticism: "It seems to me that it is not correct to speak of the 'crucified people' that 'takes away the sin of the world' and in this way 'redeems' the world. That does nothing more than religiously glorify and perpetuate the people's suffering. The people do not want to save the world with their suffering, but to be finally redeemed from their suffering and to have a humanly dignified life" ("Teología Latinoamericana," in L. C. Susin, ed., *El mar se abrió* [Santander, 2001], 209). The final phrase seems to us correct, but it does not necessarily deny that the poor, by being such, bring salvation into history. Where I would be in agreement with Moltmann is in rejecting any mechanical relation between suffering and salvation.

[85]J. Vitoria, "Una teología de ojos abiertos."

[86]Taken from M. Zechmeister, "Grito y canto."

[87]Boff and Casaldáliga have made this point. Even with all the evils it produces, present-day globalization is in fact laying the foundations for a future globalization with great human potential.

[88]Enrique Álvarez Córdova, a Salvadoran oligarch and landlord, distributed his lands to the poor small farmers on the condition that the land be owned and worked in cooperative fashion. He struggled for agrarian reform in his country and entered the ranks of the Democratic Revolutionary Front as a politician, not as a soldier. He was killed in 1979, a brilliant example of analogy.

[89]*Church: The Human Story of God* (New York, 1990), 12.

[90]This does not mean that the understanding of the traditional formula was not evolving right from the start. The formula could—and did—lead to rigorism, although in the beginning, and beyond the councils that did not fall into rigorism (Fourth Lateran and Florence, 1442), there appeared the common Christian understanding about the universal salvific will of God. One theological solution was to postulate the existence of the Church even before Christ, and thus was forged the *theologoumenon Ecclesia ab Abel*. But was it Church? Yes, from Abel on, that is, from the innocent victim, the just one, the

believer (Matt. 23:25; Heb. 11:4). Cf. C. Susin, "*Ecclesia ab Abel:* Los 'pobres' y la Iglesia al inicio del siglo XXI," *Concilium* 314 (2006): 59–69. Thus membership in the Church may be understood in terms of analogy, but with a basic criterion: wherever there are just people—innocent victims, believers, like Abel—*there, in some way*, there is Church, and there is salvation.

[91]According to *Dignitatis Humanae*, any human reality can be a place of salvation.

[92]According to *Gaudium et Spes* 3, salvation spreads out in contagious fashion: "It is human persons [body and soul, heart and conscience, intellect and will] that must be saved. . . . It is human society that must be renewed."

[93]A. Pieris, "El Vaticano II: un concilio 'generador de crisis' con una agenda no escrita," *Revista Latinoamericana de Teología* 67 (2006): 43: "The best fruit of this crisis-generating decision [the biblical soteriology rediscovered in the Council] was the *theology of liberation*, which was created by the poor of Latin America in the process of hearing and responding to the Word, as they heard it in the scriptures and in the history of their time. This was a discovery—very long overdue—of an alternative to the *theology of domination* that a non-biblical scholastic theology had produced."

[94]*Discourse in Louvain*, February 2, 1980. Romero insisted also, though not in a literal sense, on the second part of Irenaeus's dictum: *Gloria autem hominis visio Dei.* The archbishop stated: "No man knows himself as long as he has not met God. . . . How I desire, beloved brothers and sisters, that the fruit of my preaching today be that each one of us meet up with God!" (Homily of February 10, 1980, delivered two weeks before his assassination).

[95]*Marx y la Biblia* (Salamanca, 1972), 82.

[96]*¿Todavía la salvación cristiana?* II: 662, 702–3, 731–32. See also "La soteriología histórica: un modelo a partir de la teología salvadoreña (I)," *Revista Latinoamericana de Teología* 33 (1994): 292: "The poor become the ideal place for a liberating salvific praxis and the realization of God's kingdom." He mentions it again in the article quoted in this same issue.

[97]Liberation theology, because of its method—thinking on the basis of the irruption of the poor—can "paraphrase a well-known ancient dictum: *extra pauperes nulla salus*" ("Una tarea histórica: de la liberación a la apocalíptica," *Sal Terrae* [October 1995]: 718).

[98]Thinking specifically of the university, he said: "Christianity sees in the most needy, in one way or another, the redeemers of history" ("Diez años después, ¿es posible una universidad distinta?" *Estudios Centroamericanos* 324–25 [1975]: 627). And in 1979 he stated it explicitly: "The most explicit witness to the Christian inspiration of the UCA is whether it is really at the service of the people and whether in that service it lets itself be guided by the oppressed people themselves," ("Las funciones fundamentales de la Universidad y su operativización," in *Planteamiento universitario* [1989], 120). His first criterion is accepted, at least theoretically: it consists in a university's option for the poor. The second is bolder: a university should allow itself to be guided by the poor.

[99]Ellacuría, "Utopía," 173.

[100]According to *Gaudium et Spes* 19, even believers, "because of the deficiencies of their religious, moral, and social life, have concealed more than revealed the true face of God and of religion" and are one of the causes of atheism.

[101]This language of Puebla is more vigorous than that of "he has not left us, but lives in the midst of," which it also uses to mention the presence of Christ "in the midst of his Church, principally in the Holy Eucharist and in the proclamation of his word; he is present among those who come together in his name and also in the person of the pastors he has sent" (Puebla, no. 196).

[102]Such is the judgment of J. Costadoat in his article "La liberación en la cristología de Jon Sobrino," *Teología y Vida* 45 (2004): 62–84.

[103]"El pueblo crucificado: Ensayo de soteriología histórica," *Revista Latinoamericana de Teología* 18 (1989): 326.

[104]See the complete text in *Concilium* 293 (2001): 145–46.

[105]Cf. *Where Is God? Earthquake, Terrorism, Barbarity, and Hope* (Maryknoll, NY: Orbis Books, 2004), 71–105.

[106]"Misión actual," 119ff.

[107]"Cómo hablar de Dios desde Ayacucho," *Revista Latinoamericana de Teología* 15 (1988): 233–41.

[108]Cited in G. Gutiérrez, *El Dios de la vida* (Salamanca, 1994), 174 (English translation: *The God of Life* [Maryknoll, NY: Orbis Books, 1991]).

[109]"Pobres," 797.

4. The Centrality of the Kingdom of God Announced by Jesus

[1]"El reino de Dios y las parábolas de Marcos," *Revista Latinoamericana de Teología* 67 (2006): 8.

[2]Harold Pinter, in his speech upon accepting the Nobel Prize for literature, insisted on the universal dimension of present-day negativity. He spoke of "domination over the whole spectrum" in referring to the U.S. empire. This is a perversion of utopia, certainly, but still a "great narrative," and quite universal.

[3]"Hacia una cristología después de Auschwitz," *Selecciones de Teología* 58 (2001): 114.

[4]Archbishop Romero insisted also on the second part of the saying of Irenaeus, though not in its precise literal sense: "No man knows himself as long as he has not met God. . . . How I desire, beloved brothers and sisters, that the fruit of my preaching today be that each one of us meet up with God!" (Homily of February 10, 1980, delivered two weeks before his assassination).

[5]"In the face of the despotic legacy of monotheism, Marquard advocates 'the disenchanting return of polytheism': in opposition to the mono-myth of historical progress, polytheism offers 'multiple myths' in the variety of stories about the gods. The return of multiple deities and their stories will certainly be disenchanting, for in the conditions of modernity such variety will manifest itself as division of powers in the political realm and as dissension in the theories and visions about the world and about values. Human beings should not allow anything to control them completely. 'Liberate yourself, that is, take care that the powers that attack you keep one another at bay'—such is the credo of Marquard" (*Lob des Polytheismus* [Frankfurt a. M., 1996], 159), in M. Zechmeister, "¿Muerte de Dios, muerte del hombre?" *Revista Latinoamericana de Teología* 57 (2002): 244.

[6]Cf. ibid., 248–50.

[7]*Teología del Nuevo Testamento I* (Salamanca, 1972), 142 (italics in original).

[8]D. Bonhoeffer, *El precio de la gracia*, trad. de J. L. Sicre (Salamanca, 1968), 20–21 (English translation: *The Cost of Discipleship*).

[9]"Aporte de la teología de la liberación a las religiones abrahámicas en la superación del individualismo y del positivismo," *Revista Latinoamericana de Teología* 10 (1987): 9.

[10]P. Casaldáliga, "Del desencanto inmediatista a la utopía esperanzada," *Concilium* 311 (2005): 156.

[11]*Jesucristo liberador. Lectura histórico-teológica de Jesús de Nazaret* (San Salvador, 1991), 103ff. (Madrid, [4]2001; English translation: *Jesús the Liberador* [Maryknoll, NY: Orbis Books, 1993]).

[12]*Marx y la Biblia* (Salamanca, 1972), 82 (English translation: *Marx and the Bible* [Orbis Books, 1974]).

[13]In K. Rahner and K. H. Weger, *¿Qué debemos creer todavía?* (Santander, 1980), 190.

5. The Resurrection of One Crucified

[1]"One hundred thousand people die of hunger, or of its immediate consequences, every day. A child aged under ten dies every seven seconds, and every four minutes another goes blind from lack of Vitamin A. A child who dies of hunger today dies murdered" (Jean Ziegler, UN rapporteur for nutrition, interview in *El País*, May 9, 2005).

[2]"The statement that death is always the same proves as abstract as it is false": T. W. Adorno, *Dialéctica negativa* (Madrid, 1975), 371 (English ed., *Negative Dialectics* [New York: Seabury, 1973]).

[3]I have developed this in *La fe en Jesucristo. Ensayo desde las víctimas* (Madrid: Trotta, 1999; English translation, *Christ the Liberator: A View from the Victims* [Maryknoll, NY: Orbis, 2001]).

[4]1970 interview. The whole passage is splendid, still so today. It is especially illuminating on what theology is. "The world is appearance, the world is not the absolute truth. Theology is the hope that this injustice that characterizes the world will not prevail for ever."

[5]*Gesammelte Schriften* (Frankfurt: Suhrkamp, 1995), 34ff.

[6]The term "victim" is broad and complex. One can live in plenty and be victim of a dehumanizing system, to the extreme of slavery to drugs, for example. Here I am referring to human beings threatened in their basic life and dignity through oppression and repression.

[7]"I Believe in Resurrection," *Concilium* (2006/5): 121–23.

[8]I. Ellacuría, "La Iglesia de los pobres, sacramento histórico de la liberación," *ECA* 384–89 (October–November 1977): 717.

[9]*La Iglesia, fuerza del Espiritu* (Salamanca, 1978), 160 (Spanish translation of *Die Kirche im Kraft des Geistes*; English ed., *The Church in the Power of the Spirit* [London: SCM Press, 1977]).

[10]To make it more acceptable, it is said that the Christian understanding of resurrection is more believable than others because it brings together the bodily, social, and even cosmic aspects of human beings—unlike, for example, the symbols derived from Greek philosophy.

6. Helping Jesus' Legacy to Bear Fruit in the Churches

[1]There is a hermeneutical circle between the two types of Christology. To describe a person today as a "witness" of Jesus, we need to refer to some "text" on Jesus; otherwise the discussion may be driven by pure imagination or will. But to understand what texts from the past are saying—especially the real weight of the concepts—they must somehow be turned into reality. Texts from the past and realities in the present shed light on each other.

[2]"Del desencanto inmediatista a la utopía esperanzada," *Concilium* 311 (2005): 156.

[3]"El verdadero pueblo de Dios según monseñor Romero," *Estudios Centroamericanos* 392 (1981): 530.

[4]"La UCA ante el doctorado concedido a monseñor Romero," *Estudios Centroamericanos* 437 (1989): 174.

[5]Elsewhere there is also death by war, barbarism, and terrorism. We still have death by violence. There are ten homicides every day in El Salvador, and sixteen in Guatemala. The causes are different from other times. The latest is youth gang death. In any case, death remains the predominant presence.

[6]*Discurso de Lovaina*, February 2, 1980.

[7]"Monseñor Romero, un enviado de Dios para salvar a su pueblo," *Revista Latinoamericana de Teología* 19 (1990): 10. Originally published in *Sal Terrae* (December 1980): 825–32.

[8]The following words, although they are about a specific case, express better than any definition what Monseñor meant when he spoke of the "people" without the "in addition": "This week we must also mourn the death of two policemen. They are our brothers. In the face of abuse and violence, I have never spoken with partiality. With the compassion of Christ I have put myself at the side of the dead, of the victim, of the one who suffers. . . . I have said that the two policemen who died are also victims of the injustice of our system which I denounced last Sunday. One of its greatest crimes is to turn our poor against each other. The police, the workers, the peasants all belong to the poor. The evil of the system is to turn the poor against the poor. The two dead policemen are two poor men who became the victims of others, who were perhaps poor themselves, and in any case they are victims of that god Moloch, insatiable for power, for money, who in order to maintain the status quo cared nothing for the life of the peasant, or of the police, or of the soldier" (Homily of April 30, 1978).

[9]"El pueblo crucificado, ensayo de soteriología histórica," in CRT, *Cruz y resurrección: Presencia y anuncio de una iglesia nueva* (Mexico, 1978), 49–82. After his assassination it was published in *Revista Latinoamericana de Teología* 18 (1989): 305–33. See Jon Sobrino and Ignacio Ellacuría, eds., *Systematic Theology: Perspectives from Latin America* (Maryknoll, NY: Orbis Books, 1996), 257–78.

[10]"Discernir el 'signo' de los tiempos," *Diakonía* 17 (1981): 58.

[11]"El verdadero pueblo de Dios según monseñor Romero."

[12]*Palabras cristianas* (Salamanca, 2002), 98.

[13]There is not space to explore this theme fully here. It is enough to remember the third pastoral letter of Archbishop Romero and Bishop Rivera, *La Iglesia y las organizaciones populares*, August 6, 1978.

[14]See what I wrote in *Jesucristo liberador* (San Salvador, 1991; Madrid, 2001), 434–39.

[15]J. Jeremias, *Teología del Nuevo Testamento* I (Salamanca, 1974), 142 (italics in original).

[16]How the people responded is often debated, especially when in some gospel passages, near the end of his life, the people seem to abandon him and even ask for his crucifixion. It was much more complex than that, as I have discussed in "El crucificado," in J. J. Tamayo (ed.), *10 palabras claves sobre Jesús de Nazaret* (Estella, 1999), 320–22. R. Aguirre's conclusion seems historically valid: "Jesus himself never fled from the people, but from the authorities" ("Jesús y la multitud a la luz del evangelio de Juan," *Estudios Eclesiásticos* 218–19 [1980]: 1071).

[17]"Hacia una cristología después de Auschwitz," in *Selecciones de Teología* 158 (2001): 114. See also "La compasión. Un programa universal del cristianismo en la época de pluralismo cultural y religioso," *Revista Latinoamericana de Teología* 55 (2002): 25–32.

[18]"Monseñor Romero," 9.

[19]Ibid., 9–10.

[20]Ibid., 9.

[21]Ibid., 10.

[22]In this regard I want to add, as hard as it is to speak of these things, that I think Ellacuría the thinker, philosopher, critic, never credulous, knowing well the thousand and one problems it causes to place one's faith in a surpassing mystery, was attracted by a faith like Archbishop Romero's. I think it fascinated him.

[23]Pedro Casaldáliga, "Carta abierta al hermano Romero," *Revista Latinoamericana de Teología* 64 (2005): 4.

[24]"Los mártires jesuánicos en el Tercer Mundo," *Revista Latinoamericana de Teología* 48 (1999): 241–46 (English translation: "Jesuanic Martyrs in the Third World," in Jon

Sobrino, *Witnesses to the Kingdom* [Maryknoll, NY: Orbis Books, 2003], 119–33).

[25]To pursue Jesus is to "reshape realities." If I may use Zubirian language, I hope correctly, *homo religiosus* is *homo religatus*, but as *homo*, he is still an animal of realities: he goes to God by *going* to God. And he relates to God by bearing God's realities in history. "The act or acts that give us access to God are not the formally intellective acts, but those that physically and in reality, effectively bring us to God as the absolutely absolute reality" (X. Zubiri, *El hombre y Dios* [Madrid, 1984], 181). How clearly we saw this in Archbishop Romero!

[26]"El último retiro espiritual de monseñor Romero," *Revista Latinoamericana de Teología* 13 (1988): 6.

[27]See X. Alegre, "Un silencio eloquente o la paradoja del final de Marcos," *Revista Latinoamericana de Teología* 58 (2003): 3–24.

[28]D. Bonhoeffer, *El precio de la gracia*, trans. J. L. Sicre (Salamanca, 1968), 20–21 (English translation: *The Cost of Discipleship*).

[29]See what we have written in *Jesucristo liberador*, 134. See *Jesus the Liberator*, 72–74.

[30]This is not an exact formulation, because others also continued Monseñor's work and Ellacuría had already been speaking for several years in the country. In any case a UCA worker said after seeing Ellacuría on television, "No one has talked this way in our country since Archbishop Romero was murdered."

[31]"La UCA ante el doctorado concedido a monseñor Romero," *Estudios Centroamericanos* 437 (1985): 168.

[32]Ibid.

[33]Ibid.

[34]See my article "Monseñor Romero y la fe de Ignacio Ellacuría," in J. Sobrino and R. Alvarado, *Ignacio Ellacuría: "Aquella libertad esclarecida"* (San Salvador, 1999), 11–26.

Index

abundance, dehumanizing aspect of, 45–46

Adorno, 103

Allah Is Not Happy (Kouroma), 73

Angelelli, Enrique, 95

anti-kingdom, 82–88; bearing the weight of, 93–94

Augustine, 2, 41

Auschwitz, 66

Bloch, Ernst, 19, 61, 80, 105

Boff, Leonardo, 7, 120; on human insensitivity, 39

Bonhoeffer, Dietrich, 125

Brighenti, Agenor, 77

capitalism, as fundamental cause of wealth-poverty discrepancy, 38–39

Casaldáliga, Pedro, ix, xiii, 14, 19, 25, 51; on the Christian faith, 110; on freedom and justice, 57; giving names to the holy innocents, 30; intuition of, 51; on migration, 38; need for utopian hope, 81; raising and provoking resurrection, 106; on wealth, 37

Christ, transcendence of, 95–96

Christian faith, relation of, to poor, 50

Christomonism, 90

Church: created by Christ's mission, 21; current problems in, 122–23

civilization, illness of, 37

civilization of love, 14

civilization of poverty, x, 1, 14–18, 36; spirit of, 16–17; unmasking the civilization of wealth, 9–10

civilization of wealth: illness of, 35– 36; insufficient resources to provide for everyone, 9–10; producing death, 40; suspicion of, 10–14

Comblín, Jose, 14–15, 31; on the poor's vitality, 51–52

con-descendence, 118, 120–21

coproanalysis, 5, 35, 60

crucified people, 1; "always" of, 6– 7; giving a name to great majorities, 4; grace in, 8; importance of, in the present, 7–8; as negativity (sign of the times), 3–4; as positive (bringers of salvation), 4–6

death: not grasped by reason or faith, 99–100; understanding of, 99

dehumanization, 40–48; overcoming, 60–62

dehumanized world, 83–85

democracy, suspicion of, 11–12

dialectical historicization, 12–13

dialectic element, of option for the poor, 31

docetism, overcoming, 110, 121, 122–23

Doctors without Borders, 46

Dostoevsky, Fyodor. *See* Karamazov, Ivan

Ellacuría, Ignacio, 34; after Romero's death, 117–18; analytic intuition of, 51; challenging Heidegger, 3; on the civilization of poverty, 55– 56; crucified people standing for Christ crucified, 112; defending popular organization, 5; describing Romero, 109, 110–12; emphasizing taking responsibility for reality, 2–3, 8; on fear in the First World, 61; final speech of, ix, 35, 36; giving names to the holy innocents, 30; on healing civilization, x; influences on, 1; keeping alive, xi; moved by Romero's vision of the people, 16; on nature and function of Latin American churches, 76; obsessed by *justeza*, 18; on option for the poor, 19; on the people of God, 112–15; on poor appearing as signs for others, 63; premonition of, 65; on the problem of the poor, 89; on protest, 27–28, 62; on realizing the kingdom of God in history, 91; relating poor people to salvation, 71; on reversing the course of history, 36; seeing a gift in Romero, 127; on the spiritual and human wealth of the poor, 53; on the suffering servant, 72; suspicious of democracy and human rights, 11–14; on transcendence, 121; understanding of intelligence, 2; using metaphors of inverted mirror and feces analysis, 60–61; viewing Romero as model follower of Jesus of Nazareth, 121–22

engagement, as element of option for the poor, 32

ethics, ignoring, 42

eu-topia, 61, 81

evil, 72–73; affecting human spirit, 40–48; suffered by the majorities, 37–40

experience, new logic of, 51–53

faith, oriented toward transcendence, 95–97

Florensa, Teresa, 74

Francis of Assisi, 91

freedom of expression, suspicion of, 13

freedom, resulting from Jesus' resurrection, 105–6

Fukuyama, Francis, 43–44, 80

Galeano, Eduardo, 47

Gaudium et Spes, 4, 7

generosity gap, 42

Gerardi, Juan, 30, 95

Girard, René, 37

globalization, 38, 87; dehumanizing language of, 43–45

God, transcendence of, 96–97, 110, 116–21

González Faus, J. I., 71, 89

Gospels, utopia of, 81

grace, 67; opening to, 110, 126–28; praxis and, 91

Grande, Rutilio, 119

Great Lakes region (Africa), 66, 73

Gutiérrez, Gustavo, 23–24

Hillesum, Etty, 66

Himmer, Charles-Marie, 70, 89

Hinkelammert, Franz, 44

history, reversing the course of, 36

holiness, opening to, 110

Holy Fathers of Latin America, 95

holy innocents, 30

hope: coming from the poor, 61; as element of salvation, 5–6; for healing civilization, ix–x; for victims and nonvictims, emerging from Jesus' resurrection, 102–5; utopian, 80–82

Hope Principle, The (Bloch), 105

Horkheimer, Max, 102

human beings: fate of, understood in light of Jesus' fate, 100; solidarity of, 63–64

human rights, suspicion of, 11, 12–14

humility, as element of option for the poor, 32–33

hunger, eliminating, 42–43

idolatry, related to victims, 86–87

idols, taking the form of empire, 86–87

Ignatius of Loyola, 8, 34, 56, 91

intelligence, Ellacuría's understanding of, 2–3

irenicism, theological, 87–88

Jeremias, Joachim, 88, 102
Jesuanic martyrs, 29, 67, 94–95
Jesuits, on the complexity of salva-
    tion, 55–56
Jesus: Church's problem of follow-
    ing, 124–25; directing the Church,
    98; fate of, universalized, 101; as
    firstborn in journeying toward
    God, 107; following, 90–97, 123–
    24; as grace, 128; people under-
    standing God's presence in, 120–
    21; reflecting on, through Romero
    and Ellacuría, 109; relationship
    with the people, 115–16; resurrec-
    tion of, 100–8; spirit of, univer-
    salism characterizing, 92–93
John XXIII, 70, 89
John Paul II, 48
joy, resulting from Jesus' resurrec-
    tion, 106
justice, resulting from Jesus' resurrec-
    tion, 106

Kant, Immanuel, 7, 75
Karamazov, Ivan, 42, 48, 68, 75,
    100, 107, 108
kingdom of God: centrality of, 77–
    80; relation of, to anti-kingdom,
    84–85

Lercaro, Giacomo, 22, 70, 89
Levinas, Emmanuel, 103
liberation theology: addressing
    diversity of poverty, 23–24; on the
    locus of salvation, 58; need for, to
    understand Christianity, 84;
    utopia of, 81
love, resulting from Jesus' resurrec-
    tion, 106
Lumen Gentium, 98

majorities, evils suffered by, 37–40
Mark, Gospel of, x; option for the
    poor in, 20; warning against
    unreal understanding of Chris-
    tianity, 125
martyrdom, changes in concept of,
    29–30

Marx, Karl, 6, 103
Medellín, 4, 50, 80; on Christ in the
    poor, 71–72; on the Church of the
    poor, 12; discovering depth and
    diversity of the poor, 23; as fruit
    of Vatican II, 70; hope of, lost, 81
mercy, opening to, 110
messianism, 17–18
Metaphysics of Morals (Kant), 75
Metz, J. B., 26, 34, 50, 66, 82
migration, 37–38
Miranda, Porfirio, 70–71
Moltmann, Jürgen, 2, 13, 21, 44,
    107
Montesinos, Antonio, 7, 85
Muñoz, Ronaldo, 52
Mveng, Engelbert, 24–25, 55

negativity, reflecting the positive, 4
nonexistence, saving the poor from,
    28–30
nonpoor, production among, 68
nonvictims, Jesus' resurrection
    introducing hope for, 103–5

option for the poor, 19–20; depth of,
    19–25; difficulty of, 20–21, 88–
    89; framing, elements of, 31–34
ou-topia, 81

partiality, as element of option for
    the poor, 31–32
peace for the Church, 94
Péguy, Charles, 114
people: centrality of, 110; Jesus'
    relationship with, 115–16;
    theology of, 112
people of God: Ellacuría's and
    Romero's approaches to, 112–15;
    moving Romero to service, 8;
    understanding, in relation to
    kingdom of God, 97–98
Pieris, Aloysius, 55
Pinter, Harold, 48
polytheism, praise of, 87–88
poor: being in the world of, 68–69;
    centrality of, in Christianity, 88–
    90; as Church's most vigorous

challenge, 33–34; death of, as negation of fraternity, 81–82; depth of option for, 19–25; diverse dimensions of the reality of, 58–59; diversity and depth of, 22–25; finding humanity in the world of, 52; giving historical ultimacy to the mystery of God, 20–21; giving ultimacy to Church's mission, 21–22; mystery of, 72–76; mystery of God in, 75–76; no calendar for, 29, 46; positive and negative sides of the world of, 52–53; possessing values that go ignored, 62–63; relation of, to Christian faith, 50; salvation and, 48–69; saving, 25–26; saving from death, 26–27; saving from indignity, 27–28; saving from nonexistence, 28–30; shaping the process of liberation, 64; soteriological dimension of, 59; struggle of, against the anti-kingdom, 84–85; as victims, 64–68

postmodernity: discrediting the utopian vision, 80; valuing return of the idols, 87

poverty: contribution of, to salvation, 58; dehumanizing attempts to eliminate, 41–43; developing concept of, beyond socio-economics, 88–89; diverse types of, 22–25; right of, 39; saving the world, 114–15; struggle against, 6–7

praxis: grace and, 91–92; spirit and, 92–93

primordial holiness, 73–75

progress, questioning, 44

prophetic condemnation, 62

prophetic denunciation, 27

prosperity, suspicion of, 13

Puebla, 33–34; on Christ in the poor, 71–72; formulating the option for the poor, 89–90; on idols, 86; on the soteriological dimension of poor people, 59; on the suffering of the poor, 82

Rahner, Karl, 27, 34, 70, 97, 127

Ramos, Joaquín, 95

redemption: necessity of, 68; victims and, 64–68

Riobamba, bishops imprisoned in, 95

Romero, Oscar, x, xii, 4, 27, 95; attributing special force to the people, 16; on the Church suffering persecution, 94; defending popular organization, 5; Ellacuría's perceptions of, 109; experience of grace, 92; explaining the structure of his homilies, 119; giving names to the holy innocents, 30; on the glory of God, 26; on God's transcendence, 117–18, 121; on honor and seriousness, 118–19; on idols, 86; keeping alive, xi; as model follower of Jesus of Nazareth, 121–22; murder of, 67; on the people of God, 112–14; placing importance on the people, 111–12; on the poor and redemption, 64; reasons of, for giving voice to the poor, 28; reformulating the mystery of God, 70; speaking on the victims, 119; on those who disturb, 93

Rwanda, 73

Salvadoran Church, historicizing fundamental Christian tradition, 126

Salvadoran theology, leading in development of persecution and martyrdom as themes, 2

salvation: from below, need to accept, 6; characteristics of, 57; coming from the poor, 50–51; elements of, 5–6; forms of, 57–58; historical forms of, coming from the world of the poor, 60–64; logic of, in Christian and biblical tradition, 53–56; need for a new logic for understanding, 48–51; place of, 70; process of, 58; source of, 71

Schillebeeckx, Edward, 70
Sebastián, Luis de, 45, 87
Segundo, Juan Luis, 86
Sikuli, Melchisedec, 73
silence, dehumanizing aspect of, 45–46
solidarity, 14–17, 51–53, 57–60, 63–64
spirit, praxis and, 92–93
spiritual effectiveness, 15
Spiritual Exercises (St. Ignatius), 56
suffering servant, 4–5

Taubes, J., 48
theodicy, 50, 89, 97
trans-cendence, 118, 120–21
transcendence, faith oriented toward, 95–97
Traoré, Aminata, 46
Trigo, Pedro, 56
truth, overcoming degradation of, 28

United Nations Development Program, 52
United States: arrogance of, 10; empire of, 86–87; hypocrisy of, related to human rights, 11
utopia: hope and, 80–82; negated by sin's active presence, 82–83; poor transforming notion of, 61

Vallejo, César, 75
Vatican II, 22, 70
victims: Jesus' resurrection introducing hope for, 102–3; living in community with, 106–7; venerating, 65–66
Vitoria, Javier, 71

wealth-poverty discrepancy, 38–39, 46–48
weapons spending, 38
wickedness, 72–73
Wilfred, Felix, 52
world of abundance, not bringing salvation, 68–69

Zaragoza, Mayor, 48
Ziegler, Jean, ix, 37, 42
Zubiri, Xavier, 127